We A
Millions

We Are Millions

Neo-liberalism and new forms of political action in Argentina

Marcela López Levy

Latin America Bureau
LONDON

We Are Millions: Neo-liberalism and new forms of political action in Argentina
was first published by
Latin America Bureau
1 Amwell Street
London EC1R 1UL
in 2004

Latin America Bureau is an independent research and publishing organisation. It works to broaden public understanding of issues of human rights and
social and economic justice in Latin America and the Caribbean.

Editing: Martin Parmelo
Cover design: Diseño Atlántico, Buenos Aires
Cover image: Sebastian Hacher
Interior design and setting: Kate Kirkwood
Printed by J.W. Arrowsmith Ltd, Bristol

A CIP catalogue record for this book is available from the British Library

ISBN 1 899365 63 X

Contents

Acknowledgements

My main aim with this book has been to provide a space in the English-reading world for the excellent Argentinian scholarship and journalism which has analysed and commented on recent events and their historical roots. For that reason, my biggest debt is with all those who have wanted to understand how Argentina could find itself faced with yet another crisis at the beginning of the twenty-first century. I owe them an apology too, as providing a short overview has meant reducing complex works to barely lines and so I refer readers to the bibliographical notes. Needless to say, the errors arising from synthesizing are all mine.

The text was much improved by the keen querying of Anna Thomas, the speed and accuracy of Charlie Nurse and the wide-ranging and the knowledge of economics of Alan Cibils. In Buenos Aires, Renate Levy provided the means of communication, and with Claudio Levy, invaluable contacts. From Spain, Marta Levy provided a formidable cuttings service that kept me informed and permanently surrounded by newsprint.

In London, Jeff Powell shared his work on barter, while Duncan Green sent timely financial articles and reports. James Dunkerley, Claudia Hasanbegovic, Ronaldo Munk and Dennis Rodgers contributed more than they realised with their questions, advice and views.

During my visits to Argentina, many people offered their time and knowledge with great generosity, particularly Eduardo Basualdo, Sebastian Hacher, Marina Sitrin, John Jordan, Daniel Divinsky, Andrew Graham-Yooll, Federico Lorenz and Patrick

Rice. Esteban Magnani, via email, trusted me with his work on the recovered factories. Many others who helped me are mentioned in the book. Fernando Villarreal, Paula Bianco and Juana Villarreal gave me a home and *mate* throughout and provided an everyday respite from interviews and reading. A debt of gratitude to all.

I would like to thank my editor Martha Farmelo specially, for having worked tremendously hard to make the book accurate and clear, to punishing deadlines. She also contributed her knowledge and experience unstintingly. The obfuscations that remain are all my own.

Ansel Levy Dethmers' insistence on taking regular constitutionals invariably resulted in excellent thinking time, even if I had to be forcibly dragged away from the computer. Michiel Dethmers enabled me to have the time to write, a wonderful gift. To both I dedicate my efforts, a poor substitute for going and seeing for themselves, and that, I hope, is to come.

Introduction

A stroll in downtown Buenos Aires is bound to include the fabled Avenida Corrientes, alive with lights and people 24 hours a day. In 2003 it was still possible to follow the avenue towards the river at midnight and find open bookshops to browse in after coming out of a theatre or restaurant. Locals, *porteños*, can tell the façades are shabbier and the bookshops fewer, and they miss the crowds that used to throng there. Yet to the untrained eye, this is a city centre where all sorts of people come to enjoy themselves.

The avenue has other uses too. Late at night, when most people have gone home after their play and their meal, when only a few shops and news kiosks cast their lights on the broken pavement, a fleet of coaches arrives. Out step entire families who have travelled from the vast reaches of the city that spill over from the capital into the province of Buenos Aires. They are collecting anything that might be worth selling on, mostly cardboard and paper. They populate the avenue in the hundreds, filling it with their work and voices and the play of children. Several hours later they are gone, back to the neighbourhoods where there are no livelihoods. They are known as *cartoneros*, and are the embodiment of the poverty that has overtaken millions of Argentinians. Most cartoneros had jobs until a few years ago. The older ones are skilled workers, but the very young have never known regular employment – there may be as many as 40,000 working the streets of Buenos Aires alone. Their haunting presence is at odds with the uniformed waste collectors who also clean the city daily. They work from new trucks provided by the private companies contracted by the state – cleaning up the capital is worth some US$160 million a year.

Argentina in the twenty-first century appears to exist in different dimensions: in the 'official' world, there are institutions and formal instances to deal with public services from rubbish to education or health. Yet there is a growing dimension where the links between the state and people's everyday lives have been severed and a great proportion of the population has been cast adrift. In less than a generation, the country has gone from boasting the largest middle class in Latin America to having over half of the population under the poverty line.

Cartoneros are a small part of the millions who have fallen on hard times: some 16 million people were under the poverty line in 2002, while a quarter of the population could not feed itself properly. These stark figures hide the fact that until recently, the families who today find no safety net had access to education and health insurance and owned homes and businesses. One experienced cartonero explains that he now earns between five and 20 pesos (1.5 and 6.5 dollars) a day collecting cardboard, which doesn't include any contributions to a health plan. Most poor people in Latin America have never experienced social security, but the fact that for him it was the norm until recently underlines the regression in social conditions experienced in Argentina.

Argentina has seen a dramatic reduction in the social responsibility of the state, in line with neo-liberal recipes applied in Latin America. Less state spending has meant greater unemployment and fewer resources destined to social ends. Since 1982, the cash generated by the country has been sunk into ever-increasing debt payments, while wages were lower in 2003 than they were in the 1970s. Debt servicing as a percentage of exports has consistently risen, reaching 48 per cent in 2001.[1] The macro-economic 'adjustment' demanded by the International Monetary Fund (IMF) and international capital translate for the majority of the population into death by a thousand cuts – slashed social spending in education, pensions, health care – felt on the flesh of millions.

In just a few decades, Argentina has gone from being a land of immigration and promise to one of net emigration, with nearly half the economically-active population underemployed or entirely excluded from the job market. Of those who still have work, it is estimated that some 45 per cent labour in the informal sector, where they have no access to social security or health cover. There is little in the way of unemployment benefits and all social services are suffering from the reduction of state expenditure demanded by the IMF.

How did a country tipped to be a winner in the race to development find itself going backwards at such a rate? Argentina was among the ten richest nations in the world at the beginning of the twentieth century. How has it become a byword for economic meltdown in the twenty-first? Why did the upward social mobility of decades turn into a downward spiral?

Across the world, most developing countries have failed to make the 'development' leap predicted in the optimism of post-colonialism and post-war economic growth. But Argentina did manage sustained growth until the 1970s, and its economic bounty was distributed well enough to buck the Latin American trend of being the most unequal region in the world. And yet in 2003 it has become an extreme example of the widening gulf between rich and poor illustrated by the most recent UNDP (United Nations Development Programme) report, which showed that 54 countries had lower living standards in 2001 than in 1990.

Why should Argentina matter to us? Partly because the social regression experienced in Argentina mirrors processes occurring across the world, as neo-liberalism has increased inequality in and between countries. In Argentina regression has happened so fast and on such a scale that it feels as though we were watching a speeded-up horror film. Yet in the same way that special effects show us what the eye cannot catch, what is happening in Argentina makes explicit processes we all live.

The pace at which Argentina was unravelling became clear

in the explosion of popular discontent in December 2001, broadcast across the world as the nation suffered an economic meltdown that led to the biggest default on record. As historian Perry Anderson commented, '…Argentina has seen a social breakdown, amid the largest sovereign default in history, that is the equivalent for neo-liberalism of the collapse of Communism in the Soviet Union.'[2] The lead up to and effects of the crisis were cataclysmic for Argentina, but the experience speaks to millions across the world who are wary of the array of economic and political policies known to its critics as neo-liberalism.

For over a hundred years, the development ideal practiced in rich countries, and imitated with some success by Argentina, was subjection by inclusion. That is, the state bought the political and cultural domination of the poorer classes with basic services, social mobility and access to consumption. The neo-liberal model, however, was much starker in its assumptions. It dusted off the old adage of 'the poor shall always be with us' and proceeded to claim that freeing the rich from the burden of contributing to the state and its social functions was the way to prosperity. Inequality was allowed to grow while the state withdrew from its redistributive role and let the poor both increase in numbers and become irrelevant to economic functioning.

The neo-liberal capitalist is much more short-term in his or her need for profit and more likely to rely on speculation, which does not need productivity but rather thrives on instability. Expanding markets is not a priority, but repressing those left out of the financial loop certainly is. Neo-liberal policies have contributed to the ever greater dependence of developing nations: on loans, investment, and imports from the rich world. Dependency is a concept fallen out of favour in economics, but it is an apt description of the process. Poor nations also became the battlefield for market conquest and trade wars between richer nations. In 2001 and 2002, the US Treasury Department paraded representatives quoted in the media saying that Argentina's collapse wasn't important. Of course it didn't matter to them, because relatively few US interests were compromised (and the IMF had ensured its loans in 2001 had been used to repay debts with US financers). Instead, the largest losses were taken by European firms.

What has happened in Argentina is a warning to the rest of the world that breakdown could happen anywhere, even in the developed world. In fact it already has – witness Russia – but the West has not analysed the importance of that collapse. Even though US Treasury Secretary Paul O'Neill would have Argentina to be 'a friggin' banana republic', it is the most developed country in the region and among the 40 most developed in the world. But now, thanks to neo-liberal reform, millions of Argentinians live in poverty. The biggest lesson from Argentina is that it is possible in the twenty-first century for human development to be undone. 'Progress' is not a given. It has to be fought for and defended.

Although Argentina's panorama is bleak, the hopeful lesson is that people have grasped the challenge. People have taken to the streets in a manner that reaches beyond protest: they have demanded a complete restructuring of the state and of social relations and have volunteered to be part of making change happen. The population has become more aware of the mental and economic chains which bind them and are in the process of trying to break them – or at the very least, have discovered how to rattle them loudly.

A range of innovative social movements has arisen out of the economic crisis which began to bite in the mid 1990s, and their strategies and actions are valuable resources for those concerned with the impact of neo-liberal policies on societies world wide. These movements are described in some detail, although in the limiting context of their recent appearance. To understand what compelled them to act, it is necessary to take a look at the economic conditions of the 1990s and the social responses to neo-liberalism that preceded them. And to illuminate how Argentina got to neo-liberalism, some history is needed. The historical notes are focused and synthesized, and highlight aspects of a much bigger and complex story that can be pursued in an array of history books, a few published in English.[3]

This book begins with the tumultuous events of late 2001 and early 2002 and in Chapter One gets behind the headlines of the crisis to see what it meant for Argentinians. Chapter Two provides a brief historical background to the economic and political actors in Argentina and reviews the implantation of the neo-liberal model and its full realisation under the dictatorship that began in 1976, and covers the period up to the economic crisis of 1989. Chapter Three takes up the story in the 1990s, with the specific policies that led to the most recent default, while also looking at the social and political actors who began to question the economic model, as more and more people were excluded from its benefits. Chapter Four describes a few of the many and vibrant social organisations that arose in the late 1990s and after the explosion of 2001 – the collective and individual responses to the penury and violence that has been wrought upon people, and their path from consumers to creators of political ideas and actions. Brief conclusions attempt to convey the partial and emerging judgements being made within Argentina about what these recent experiences mean. Finally, a postscript reviews the style and content of President Néstor Kirchner's first 100 days in office.

Notes

1 UNDP, http://www.undp.org/hdr2003/indicator/cty_f_ARG.html
2 Anderson, P. 'The Cardoso Legacy', *London Review of Books*, Vol. 24 No. 24, December 12 2002.
3 Three good general accounts are *A history of Argentina in the twentieth century* by Luis Alberto Romero, Pennsylvania State University Press, 2002; *Argentina, 1516–1987: from Spanish colonization to Alfonsín* by David Rock, University of California Press, revised edition, 1989; and *Argentina, a short history*, by C.M. Lewis, Oneworld, 2002. For a collected volume, see *Argentina since independence,* edited by Leslie Bethell, Cambridge University Press, 1993.

1
The Argentinazo

'The politicians have stolen our future.'
The Guardian, April 25 2002[1]

The roar of the people and their pots and pans

December 19th 2001: across Argentina, crowds had been looting supermarkets for days. At nearly 11 o'clock on that hot summer night, President Fernando de la Rúa went on TV to declare a state of siege, suspending all constitutional rights and guarantees. With hindsight he admitted it would have been better to let the press office make the announcement. Instead, he personally faced the people through the cameras and condemned 'the enemies of order and the Republic who are taking advantage to try to sow discord and violence…' The man who had stated in days previous that 'there is no cause for alarm' at the social situation in the country took off his glasses on air to give emphasis to his words, much as an exasperated parent would confront a recalcitrant teenager.

After two years of government so weak it was hardly noticeable, and with the country on the edge of a breakdown, his reprimand sparked off the largest unplanned march on the seat of presidential power ever seen in Argentina. It was the last straw from a president who had proved unable to keep any of his promises and had led the country to the brink of default – by default – with an indecisiveness that protracted the dire economic state of the nation.

The rumble of discontent became audible – anger at his words, at his inability to act, at the audacity to declare a state of siege in the face of people's desperation. Less than a minute after he spoke the words, scattered individuals began banging metal pots on their balconies and in their windows. Slowly, as it spread, the banging of pots and pans became more distinct and insistent as groups of people moved to the streets. Entire families poured out of their homes, meeting at corners, still banging, metal on metal. More went down to join them, the crowds swelling to thousands as ever increasing groups of enraged citizens marched towards the city centre in Buenos Aires and onto public squares across the land. There were people of all ages, moved to action of their own volition. There was no call from a political party, a union or the media. The only banner on the streets was the light blue and white national flag.

The uprising drew on the collective knowledge of '*puebladas*', peoples' rebellions, although recent ones in the 1990s and earlier historical examples were often violent, sporadic and localised. This protest was peaceful and occurred over and over again during the next several weeks. Earlier in December, the banging of pots and pans that preceded the countdown to the demonstrations had been increasing in intensity. These demonstrations were known as '*cacerolazos*', where *cacerolas* (pots and pans) become a verb (*cacerolear*), an act of assertion and repudiation. The events of the 19th and 20th of December would be known at the biggest *cacerolazo* of them all, a country-wide protest remembered as the *Argentinazo*, when what was at stake was the nature and future of Argentina.

People's frustration overflowed and they began to express their thoughts and feelings in vociferous profanity. Swear words are a common communication short cut and among the angry and frustrated epithets, many original chants emerged that night: '*boludo, boludo, el estado de sitio te lo metés en el culo*' (you bastard, you bastard, up yours with the state of siege). Another phrase taken up by young and old became the signature tune of that hot summer, and resonated throughout the world: '*que se vayan todos, que no quede ni uno solo...*' (out with the lot of them, every single one) – the corrupt politicians, the interfering IMF, the rapacious foreign companies and the national economic elite.

The Argentinazo began late on the 19th and continued through the next day. Citizens showed they were not going to be cowed by the threat of repression and took to the streets to show where the politicians' mandate truly rested. Economy Minister Domingo Cavallo resigned at about 1am on December 20th and the crowds in the Plaza de Mayo demanded that President de la Rúa follow suit. Throughout the 20th, people returned to the streets wanting to defy the state of siege, to participate in whatever would happen next, to be part of history in the making. It took a whole day of street battles between mounted policemen lobbing gas canisters into the crowds and young men returning fire with stones for de la Rúa to leave the presidential offices, the *Casa Rosada*, in a helicopter.

On the 20th many watched the events on TV, waiting to see what would happen, wondering whether to risk taking to the streets. Others had already decided and from the early morning on, women in suits, men with briefcases, housewives and grandparents and all sorts of people congregated in the Plaza de Mayo. In one corner of the square the mounted police regrouped between attempts to disperse the crowds. In their recounting of events, many people said afterwards that it was the TV coverage of police horses rearing over the Madres de Plaza de Mayo (see Glossary) that provoked the outrage that brought them out on the streets.

For many, this was the first time they were part of a demonstration. Nobody had asked them to come and most did not imagine the level of repression President de la Rúa would unleash upon them. One newcomer to protest was Gustavo Benedetto, who was killed by a lead bullet shot from inside the offices of a bank near Plaza de Mayo. A year on, writer Naomi Klein recorded,

'Benedetto loved reading books about history and economics. According to his older sister, Eliana, "he wanted to understand how such a great country could have ended up in such a mess."

[...]

The mood ... is one of mourning, nowhere more so than at the corner of Avenida de Mayo and Chacabuco, in front of the head-quarters of HSBC Argentina, a hulking 28 storeys of Darth Vader-tinted glass. It was on this same piece of asphalt that 23-year-old Gustavo Benedetto fell to the ground exactly a year earlier, killed by a bullet that came from inside the bank. The man charged with the murder – who had been in a group of police officers caught on video shooting through the bank's tinted glass – is Lieutenant Jorge Varando, chief of HSBC's building security. He is also a retired elite military officer who was active during the 1970s, when 30,000 Argentines were disappeared, many of them kidnapped from their homes, brutally tortured and then thrown from planes into the muddy waters of the Rio de la Plata.'[2]

Of the 29 people who died in those 48 hours, most were killed by the security forces, making it clear that standing up to a repressive state carries real risks. Hundreds more were arrested, intimidated, and injured.

The driving force for this uprising was largely a gut reaction, an intuitive grasp of the underlying problems of the country, too long hidden under wishful thinking and illusions. The fabric of lies woven during the 1990s – when consumerism was conspicuous and the poor who couldn't afford it were ignored – was left in tatters. It was a heady time steeped in a sense of shared destiny when people bypassed politics as usual. They protested for several weeks while the political establishment reasserted its control, after five successive presidents ruled during two weeks in late December and the first days of January. The pots and pans expressed the palpable anger which hit the streets. It was a spontaneous uprising nobody had called for and no organisation could take credit for. The moment of overflowing rage is remembered now as the *Argentinazo*, the time when the majority said, '*Enough*'!

From riches to rags

Argentina's political temperature had been rising since December 1st, when Economy Minister Domingo Cavallo announced state intervention over private bank accounts, limiting cash withdrawals to 250 pesos (or dollars) a week. This restriction was immediately dubbed the *corralito*, literally small enclosure, also popularly the name for a playpen. Argentinians were being treated like infants by a government without real solutions. The reaction was a prolonged rattling of the cage, partly in desperation and partly in fury.

Most Argentinians receive their salaries and pay their rent, utilities, food – some even buy homes – with cash. Suddenly there was hardly any money flowing through the system, which affected people at all social levels. Everyone from shoe salespersons to domestic workers were not paid, so many of them, in turn, could not pay their debts, buy Christmas presents or put food on the table.

Although it was only known much later, it surprised no one that de la Rúa himself had been caught with over US$1 million in the corralito. His plight was put down to ineptitude, certainly not an ethical stand to be 'with the people'. The limits on bank withdrawals were implemented after massive capital flight took place throughout 2001; it intensified in the last months of the year, haemorrhaging some US$15,500 million out of the country. The bulk of the money exiting Argentina belonged to very wealthy individuals and companies, the latter mostly foreign as national capital has traditionally been kept outside the country, in permanent 'flight'. Banks have not been able to show reliable balance sheets for that year and the suspicion persists that they spirited millions out of the country as they saw devaluation loom.

It was not only bank vaults where shelves were being cleared. In December 2001, in supermarkets across the country, looting – some organised and some spontaneous – began to add to the panic. Not only President de la Rúa watched in horror as the looting was broadcast on TV. The population at large understood that the situation could not be contained any longer and those outside the country wondered how Argentina's downfall had come to pass. Everyone remembered the frantic ransacking which announced the fall of Radical President Raúl Alfonsín in 1989. That time there were 14 deaths, 80 wounded and 14 arrested. In 2001, looting again resulted in fatalities.

The corralito and looting precipitated the massive street demonstrations that culminated in the resignation of de la Rúa and seven-day President Adolfo Rodríguez Saá who followed him. The dire situation also gave life to the continuous *cacerolazos* in 2002, which in turn became the seedbed of a new social phenomenon, the neighbourhood assemblies. But the fuse which ignited the explosion that was the Argentinazo had been smouldering for years. It was fuelled by people's despair at not being in the first world, at being in Latin America after all, at finding themselves in crisis again but in a much worse condition, worn down by 25 years of economic instability. The Argentinazo reminded people of the economic crises the country had suffered throughout the twentieth century. As they contemplated the ruins of the country, they lost confidence in their leaders, although conversely they regained it in themselves. That surge in confidence occurred even as the country fell deeper and deeper into crisis.

The new year saw yet another president in office, Eduardo Duhalde, the Peronist loser of the 1999 elections. After much backroom negotiating, he was selected by Congress to finish de la Rúa's term. As expected, one of his administration's first measures was to devalue the peso. The results were unpredictable and so made people fearful, but they could at least be certain that they had made their deposits in dollars, and so would be able to ride out the peso's loss of value. Nobody had bargained for the next policy decision: the *corralón* (big playpen), which consisted of the forced conversion from dollars to pesos of bank accounts at a rate established by the government.

Many Argentinians call the year following the Argentinazo the worst in the country's history. '*Capicúa*' numbers, palindromes, are meant to bring good luck in Argentina, and everyone checks their bus ticket to see if the number mirrors itself. Yet the capicúa year 2002 could well break that particular superstition. It was Argentina's own annus horribilis, when by the government's own estimation, one person fell under the poverty line every four seconds. More than five million households were poor, accounting for 22.3 million people. Of these, 11.9 million people were extremely poor, a euphemism for the fact that they were hungry. All told, 61 per cent of the population was poor or extremely poor. Trade unions demanded a raise in salaries to combat the inflation that reached 45 per cent during 2002, but was closer to 80 per cent if only basic foodstuffs are counted. After the January 2002 devaluation, Buenos Aires went from being the most expensive capital in Latin America to the fourth cheapest in the world, just three away from Asunción, capital of Paraguay and, to many Argentinians, a byword for backwardness.[3]

The anger expressed during the Argentinazo had deep roots and the specific events leading up to it had echoes in the past. Argentinians perceived the crisis as the culmination of a long historical process that included the policies of the 1990s, but had its antecedents in the economic era consolidated by the dictatorship of 1976. Moreover, the social response of revulsion toward Argentina's political institutions and representatives drew on an entire twentieth century of only fitful democracy and an unsteady deterioration in the hopes of becoming part of the first world.

Argentina was cursed with spectacular success during the late nineteenth and early twentieth centuries. During the twentieth century that economic development supported social mobility and an ever-expanding middle class. The country was, and remains, the most developed in Latin America, and for a time figured among the richest nations in the world. Enough progress was achieved for Argentinians to not-so-jokingly refer to themselves as the best of the continent and to assume a misplaced sense of superiority over the rest of Latin America.

After being battered by dictatorship and economic instability for the best part of 20 years, the sense of having made it peaked during the 1990s, when dollar-peso parity gave Argentinians both an inflated purchasing power and a sense of having put chaos behind them. On the surface the country regained its aspirations: it felt part of the worldwide fashion of market economics and trumpeted its benefits. Yet the possibility of consumerism for a few was based on an over-valued currency, and on a precarious and tacit accord that allowed those in power to pilfer in return for the stability. After the experience of hyperinflation, a reliable currency that was worth the same year in year out became invaluable to Argentinians. The new peso allowed the shrinking middle class to travel, access credit and feel part of the first world. But there was nothing for the increasing number of people left outside the charmed circle, who protested more and more vocally, but to no avail. The reigning economic model had a place for those not in the financial system: out in the cold beyond state concern, to fend for themselves.

So the world's forecast of greatness for Argentina never truly materialised, and on the contrary, in the late 1990s Argentina became stuck in a downward economic spiral. In 2001 it became clear that the way to achieve greatness had not been found in over 100 years. Argentina fell to earth with a thump and found itself at the bottom of a long Latin American conti-nent, one among many nations struggling to stem poverty.

Instead of fulfilling the great shared expectations, the country was at risk of losing its place in the world.

During 2001 the country was mesmerised by the rising level of 'risk' assigned to Argentina by foreign investors and banks. Everybody watched and few understood what the figures of *riesgo país* (country risk premium) stood for in practice. Country risk rating is all about the standing of a nation among the international investment community, from the large creditors to the individual speculators who move 'hot' money around the globe in seconds. Yet its symbolic meaning, as the numbers stared back from the front page of the newspapers, was that the risk-rating escalation stood not only for the falling confidence of the world in Argentina, but also for the fear of Argentinians themselves who watched their fortunes spiral out of their control once more.

The concept of risk, in Argentina, is one filled with justifiable foreboding. Since the early 1970s, financial insecurity had been the norm, the result of attempts to maximise profits while reducing the power of salaried workers, and also a consequence of international changes in financing develop ment.[4] At each juncture of crisis, a few benefited from the possibilities of speculation, those with the wherewithal to not care about the outcomes. For the majority, each new downturn brought deep and well-founded panic: will I have a job? Will I have enough money to buy food? Will my savings be safe? In 1976, 1985 and 1991, wages were frozen; in 1975 and 1985 inflation skyrocketed and in 1989 and 1990 reached 'hyper' levels, so incomes hardly covered the basic necessities of the majority; between 1974 and 1983, political or social dissent was met with extra-judicial murder; in 1990 and 2002 the savings of private individuals were confiscated by the state and returned in part, in bonds or not at all. The fears were not idle.

During the 1990s there had been a collective illusion that the country had put its turbulent past behind it, that stability, or at least a strong currency and low inflation, were there to stay. The self-deception was so thorough that the majority of small and medium savers left their money in the banks when it was in the public domain in mid-2001 that companies and foreign investors were withdrawing their cash in the millions. They believed in the foreign banks where their money was held in dollars; it was too painful to contemplate that stability could be a mirage upon the same quicksand which had swallowed them before.

To understand what has been lost, it is necessary to know something more of what Argentina achieved in the twentieth century, and what destiny it had hoped to fulfil.

Notes

1   Goñi, U. 'Cashless and Hopeless on the streets of Buenos Aires,' *The Guardian*, April 25 2002, http://www.guardian.co.uk/international/story/0,3604,690059,00.html

2   Klein, N. 'Argentina, a new kind of revolution,' *The Guardian*, January 25 2003

3   See government web site, http://www.trabajo.gov.ar/programas/sociales/jefes/files/impacto_enlapobreza_octubre.pdf

4   Changes linked to the international rise of finance capital, displacing the industrial capital which had dominated till then (after the Bretton Woods fixed exchange rate system was abandoned in 1973). Monetarism was the ideology; total financial deregulation was the policy (financial liberalization). Rather than allowing capital to be allocated internationally to its most productive use, it gave rise to the 'international casino economy', where new markets were outbidding each other to receive capital at rates that were way too high, and for periods way too short, to be able to be used for productive investment. Economist Alan Cibils, personal communication

2
Great Expectations

Las penas y las vaquitas van por la misma senda...
Las penas son de nosotros, las vaquitas, son ajenas.
Atahualpa Yupanqui, El Arriero

Get rich not very quick

Argentina began its 'European' history as the Spanish colony full of not very much. It is named after the silver it never had, and what was imagined to be emptiness turned out to be full of 'Indians' who could defend themselves against invasion (for three hundred years). The province of River Plate was important for its port, the place from which the silver of Potosí (now Bolivia) left for Europe. A genocidal war was fought against the indigenous people once it was clear that inland from Buenos Aires were vast stretches of richly fertile soil, the *pampas*. To this day the province of Buenos Aires contains some of the most profitable arable land in the country – a land of plenty used mostly to produce for export.

It had taken three centuries for Europeans to realise that with no obvious natural resource to plunder, work would be required to profit from the bountiful soil. To make the land productive required people (Indians didn't count) and capital. In the nineteenth century Argentina produced grains, beef and wool, its signature exports. The UK was its major investor. By 1913, 20 per cent of UK capital overseas was invested in Latin America, and half of that in Argentina.[1]

Risk and its high returns were familiar concepts to those capitalists and liberal investors. The province of Buenos Aires is remembered in London for defaulting on a one million pounds debt held by Barings Bank in 1820. The national Argentinian government nearly bankrupted the Barings Brothers in 1890, although the business nevertheless survived to invest unwisely 150 years later.[2] In the early 1800s, as in the 1970s, economic success in Europe meant too much cash and not enough places to invest. In spite of the setbacks, in the late nineteenth and early twentieth centuries, Argentina attracted large amounts of European investment and immigration. Over six million Europeans, mainly Italians and Spaniards, arrived at the shores of the Rio de la Plata, most between 1860 and 1914.[3]

In spite of the serious economic and cultural challenges presented by mass immigration, Argentina began the twentieth century as a country of great promise. Its exports made it wealthy in national terms and the small population, with an increasing proportion of Europeans, was tipped for great things. The most often asked question in the history of Argentina is: what went wrong?

Yet not all predictions of future greatness need come true, or not on the hoped for scale. It is true that Argentina presented great potential, and considering the constraints (both external international economic developments and internal social and political realities), it realised a good many of its expectations. It became the country in Latin America with the highest standard of living, with the best education system, with the largest middle class. But it was not Canada, and the dream remained that it should have been.[4]

It is not as simple as 'what went wrong', as though some natural disaster had swept Argentinian dreams of glory away. There were cumulative choices made by those governing and those governed, and these resulted in a nation where the state was more likely to rule for the few than for the many, and where democratic institutions remained too weak to mediate for the common good in the conflicts between social sectors. The malleability of the state in Argentina made high office a battleground where particular economic interests have either carried the day or brought government to a standstill with their stalemates.

Land, capital and workers

A country the size of western Europe, Argentina spans tropical forest, deserts and the highest mountain in the Americas, and is the nearest country to the southern pole. Its expanse includes many geographical differences subsumed into two main categories: the capital and the rest. Historically, metropolitan Buenos Aires has been a domineering part of the whole, and now contains a third of the country's population and much of its wealth. In addition, up to two thirds of the population live in Buenos Aires province, the surrounding pampa and nearby coastal provinces. The rest of the country became, in imagination and economically, 'outlying' to these areas. The extremes of wealth and access to power found between the coastal 'centre' and the provinces is also found within regions. The province of Buenos Aires has both the most powerful landowners and the largest shantytowns in the country.

National economic power has historically been concentrated in the landed oligarchy that accumulated its wealth through exporting raw materials to Europe: first wool, then cereals and meat. Today Argentina has become an important exporter of (genetically modified) soya, edible oils and cattle, still. They lost direct control of the government at the beginning of the twentieth century, but have retained enormous political weight, either by influencing government, by helping to run it, as during the last dictatorship, or by using their economic might to dictate events.

Since the early days of export success in the late nineteenth century, the wealth of the establishment has become synonymous with ostentation, keeping assets in foreign accounts, and a dedicated lack of interest in the national development of the

The economic establishment in Argentina

Land in Argentina has historically been owned by many, although large extensions predominate, and these are concentrated in relatively few families who have kept their landed wealth for two centuries. Researcher Eduardo Basualdo comments on how time consuming it is to find out who owns what. His painstaking work points to a much larger concentration of land ownership than appears at first glance from the land registry, since hidden behind the names of many different companies lay only a handful of people who prefer to keep their vast landholdings cut up into small parcels for tax purposes.

The export-led phase of growth in the late nineteenth and early twentieth centuries was managed by an agrarian elite based geographically in Buenos Aires province that went on to invest in industrial interests such as meat-packing. The wealth extracted from the land allowed the diversification of economic interests, primarily financial with some industrial ventures. From the early days of export success, money earned in international currencies has been kept abroad by these wealthy citizens who do not trust the country of their birth and bounty. These groups became so self-sufficient as to not need the rest of society, an attitude that persisted even when national development required their participation.[5]

It was this sector which benefited most during the last military dictatorship. The man in charge of instituting economic policy, José Martínez de Hoz, was part of the landed class and had represented their powerful association, the Sociedad Rural Argentina (Rural Association of Argentina). The concrete mechanisms through which they greatly increased their fortunes in the 1970s changed in the 1980s and 1990s, but their ability to use the state to make guaranteed profits only increased. At the beginning of Menem's mandate in 1989 they were offered the Economy Ministry and from 1991 they took part in the buying spree offered by privatisation which so benefited them and their international partners.

country. National producers are not hampered by social or national responsibility. They work to generate profit and in their minds the fact that nine million Argentinians go hungry when agricultural exports are estimated to be able to feed 300 million people only reflects the worldwide reality that hunger is caused by human decisions rather than natural causes. They are not to blame if the state cannot balance the needs of all its citizens. But there are times when their behaviour has gone beyond indifference to disdain. During bouts of high inflation, as supermarkets were emptied by anxious consumers, they speculated with their produce, withholding basic foodstuffs from the internal market to benefit from ever-higher prices.

The oligarchy was displaced from government by the emergence of the Unión Cívica Radical, commonly known as the Radicals or UCR. The party was founded in the early twentieth century and represented middle-class interests, and the party's rise coincided with universal male suffrage. Simultaneously, the first three decades of the century saw further economic expansion and immigration. The workers began to organise for their rights, some of which were incorporated into law, although not into practice.

The military first took power in a coup in 1930. During that decade, military governments expanded the development of industry while at the same time using repression to keep workers under control. The way the working class was treated comes over in the interviews collected by historian Daniel James. A factory operator remembers: 'working people weren't worth anything, and we got no respect from those who controlled everything,' explained Don Ramiro.[6]

Recognition for the working class was to come from an unlikely source: the same military, when Colonel Juan Domingo Perón began to use his position at the head of the Ministry of Labour to strengthen the trade unions. Perón came to power after another coup, in 1943. He went on to become the defining figure in Argentinian politics of the second half of the twentieth century. His own political line remained hazy: nationalist, anti-communist, impressed with the all-encompassing vision of fascism, anti-imperialist and populist, champion of the working class – all these definitions applied to him. During almost two terms in power, he brought together a wide range of social forces, excluding the oligarchy and the left. Both the rich and the socialists found his popularity with the politically excluded anathama.

In the twenty-first century, the cultural weight of Peronism continues to amaze. A beautiful sunny day is still known as a '*día peronista*' (Peronist day) and the mystique surrounding Perón and his wife, Evita, lives on. Yet Perón's success in establishing himself as an iconic politician arose from concrete measures. The main one was a conscious and concerted effort to win the support of the working and lower-middle classes by improving their standard of living and providing controlled access to political power via the unions. He also relied on the charisma of Evita, who did elicit something akin to religious fervour, cemented with material gifts bestowed by her foundation. Finally, he benefited enormously from the banning of his movement by the military who ousted him in 1955, and the repression they used to enforce the ban. It was that more than anything which sealed the loyalty of the lower classes who had felt championed by him. They created a martyr where the infinitely flexible Perón might have disappointed his supporters, had he been given the chance to negotiate with the political establishment that overthrew him.

To understand his importance, it is worth remembering what some guerrillas said in the 1970s when they were asked why they were militants in Peronist rather than left-wing organisations: 'because Peronism has the working class.' The first Peronist government brought the lower-middle and working class into the political arena and ensured that rights to fair pay, holidays and sick leave were implemented. Women got the vote in 1947 with intense lobbying by Evita. Peronism meant the emancipation of the newly-constituted population, millions of by then second generation immigrants. The population had grown from under two million in 1870 to almost eight million in 1914 and nearly 16 million in 1947.[7] The social importance of the reforms and the rhetoric of Peronism were immense. The working class gained in confidence and self-respect.

The reduced history of Peronism

Tomes have been written about Peronism. Given the impossibility to do justice to them, a taster of Perón's entry in the 'Who's Who' of Argentinian history might read like this:

Perón, Juan Domingo (1895–1974): The military man who rose to power after the coup of 1943. Served in Italy and admired Mussolini. The Minister of Labour (1943–1945) who supported the workers. Vice-president and Minister of War, 1945. The man who agreed with everyone. Relationship with radio soap star Eva Duarte. Arrest by the army to curb his power, 1945. Eva and the workers take to the streets demanding his freedom. He speaks to thousands from the balcony of the Casa Rosada. Founds political party (Partido Peronista) as a 'third way' between communism and fascism. Swept to power in elections, 1946. Re-election by landslide, 1951. Evita's death in 1952. Both worshipped by working and lower-middle classes. Hated by the upper-middle class and oligarchy. Overthrown by coup in 1955. Peronism made illegal in Argentina. Exile in Paraguay, Venezuela, Panama, Franco's Spain. Decisive influence from afar over national politics via trade unions (1955-1972). Peronist armed groups formed and defeated in struggles against dictatorships (1955-1969). New radical left Peronist groups emerge including Montoneros, from 1968. His party allowed to stand in elections of 1973 and wins. Perón returns in 1973 and is elected President. Death, 1974.

(Peronism): After Perón's death the presidency falls to María Isabel Martínez, his third wife. Mandate cut short by coup of ||||➡

1976. Trade unions (mostly Peronist) declared illegal once more. Union resistance helps end military dictatorship in early 1980s. Peronism loses first fair election ever, 1983. Internal conflict in part for the soul of Peronism, 1980s. Carlos Menem wins internal Partido Justicialista, ('PJ', as the party is now known) election for presidency, 1988. Menem voted president, 1989. Appoints oligarchic cabinet, departing from historic Peronism. Re-elected after defeating inflation, 1995. Loses 1999 election to centre-left Alianza. Argentinazo and power vacuum lead to Eduardo Duhalde (defeated PJ candidate in 1999 elections) taking power January 1st 2002. Epic Menem vs Duhalde battle for the PJ ends in certain defeat for Menem (and his withdrawal) in 2003 elections and victory for Duhalde's candidate, Néstor Kirchner. PJ becomes cabal of provincial governors.

Perón was displaced by yet another military coup, in 1955, a self-proclaimed revolution. The conflict set up by the violent dislodging of Peronism would play itself out over another 20 years. The military and sections of the oligarchy pitted themselves against the organised workers and sectors of national industry that benefited from the state-led development implemented by all governments since the 1930s. For the economically powerful, reducing the strength of the unions became something of an obsession. In spite of their increasing corruption and connivance, the unions helped workers keep their share of national income until the beginning of the 1970s, in what became known as 'Peronist resistance'. The struggle confronting different economic interests was to be damaging for society, even though the economy performed well, again until the early 1970s.

Foreign exchange was still generated by agricultural exports and those were controlled by the same oligarchic minority. But manufacturing and services became increasingly important, as import substitution, as the process of industrialisation was known, gained ground. The workers and also industry welcomed the presence of the state in the economy as a safeguard against the interests of agribusiness, the banks and multinationals.[8]

Between 1955 and 1973, different military regimes were interspersed with short democratic interludes, all with quite distinct agendas and backers within the economic elites. The common thread was the lack of a clear programme of government which could be sustained over time. The lack of support for any one political project made people disillusioned with democracy and many came to prefer order (even if military) to democratic freedom and disagreement, strong government over fruitless debate. Frustration and a sense of stagnation emanated from the political stalemate between powers without majority backing but with enough might to veto anyone else's initiatives. Politics seesawed between civilians and the military with none able to rule constructively.

Meanwhile, the economy did well, although it did not live up to the great expectations Argentinians placed upon it. In fact, agricultural exports had a prolonged improvement from the early 1960s until the 1980s, when productivity was multiplied by four and the accompanying industrialisation (of food processing, agricultural inputs and machinery mostly) became an important part of the national economy. The only complaint of exporters was the amount they contributed to the running of the state. They openly championed not paying tax and contributed to a national attitude that paying tax was for mugs. The impact of the most powerful economic interests evading taxes was felt both politically and in terms of development: it proved that the state could not, or would not, harness private interests for the common good. Yet in spite of oligarchic complaints, state-led industrialisation was succeeding in expanding the manufacturing base and creating economic growth on a scale never seen again. There was sustained growth, hand in hand with distribution across the population, and upward social mobility became the norm. In spite of stop-start cycles in the economy, wealth had grown, the middle class had expanded and islands of progressive thought were created in universities and among left-wing groups.

The political economy of the 1950s and 1960s was a partial solution to development, based on repression. Deficits in the country's democracy and the culture of confrontation between social sectors made Argentinians aware that they were not fulfilling their promise. 'Saviours of the nation' came and went, but censorship and authoritarianism stayed.

The coup of 1966 turned up the repression and society's resistance became more widespread. The contradictions and tensions in society built up to breaking point and in May 1969, a popular uprising remembered as '*el Cordobazo*' brought the differences into the open. Students and workers who were organised in new independent union structures protested amid bullets. The culmination of stoppages, strikes and protests was to have been a general strike on May 30 to protest military repression, murders of students and workers, and economic measures. But on the 29th a demonstration in the city of Córdoba foreshadowed the state of the nation. Here is how Agustín Tosco, one of the main organisers, remembered the day.

'There was no spontaneity, no improvisation, no group was stranger to the resolutions adopted. The unions were organised and so were the workers. We fixed the places to meet, how to march. The 29th dawned a tense day. [...] The people's explosion takes place, the rebellion against the murderers, against the attacks. The police retreats. Nobody is in control of the situation. It is the people, the grassroots, who fight. Everyone helps. The support of the whole population occurs everywhere. It is everyone's consciousness on the streets, against prohibitions. No more guardians, or usurpers of power, or collaboration.'[9]

El Cordobazo heralded the intensified resistance of the population to the military. In 1973 the political game was opened up. Peronism was allowed to stand for elections for the first time since 1955. The PJ won the elections that called for

Perón's return that year. New elections took him to the presidency, but an old and conservative Perón died before people could judge how he might have governed. The ideological extremes within both the Peronist movement and society fed an armed struggle in which the state had the overwhelming advantage of force. The stage was set for a clash of radically different visions of social change, neither of which had majority support.

The darkest hour: the 1976 coup

The chaos of the early 1970s seemed entirely home grown: the cult of Perón, his dramatic return from exile, and the split in the movement he founded. He sided with the right-wing in power and expelled the left-wing of mostly young militants willing to give their lives for revolution. A death squad run from the Ministry of Social Welfare brought brutal repression to the left. Known as the Triple A (the Anticommunist Alliance of Argentina), its appearance showed that the fierce battle being fought for the hearts and minds of Argentinians existed beyond Peronism and had found a place in the wider Cold War scenario, in a Latin America shaken by guerrilla revolutions and military counterinsurgency. Political murders and the first disappearances (where civilians were taken by police or the military and could not be traced through the legal system) were numerous between 1974 and 1976. Only a few of the disappeared returned. The vast majority were murdered.

The repressive regime of María Estela 'Isabelita' Martínez, Perón's third wife, oversaw the last year of Peronist government, which was characterised by social and economic chaos. Financial steps taken in mid-1975 included devaluation and an increase of up to 200 per cent in the cost of public services. These measures unleashed trade union resistance, although strikes were unable to stop the loss in value of salaries and the increasing inflation. The first experience of high inflation caused a shock of food shortages and speculation not seen before, and left the country reeling with insecurity and anxiety. Argentina seemed to be spinning out of control, and Isabelita clearly wasn't in charge.

Hence the generalised relief when the military took power again in the name of 'Western, Christian values' (their capitals) 'to restore order' on March 24th 1976. Except that, both socially and economically, order came at a huge cost. The three armed forces had already been part of the paramilitary war without quarter against the left, and their control of government ensured that there was nowhere to hide for those who disagreed with them. The country was plunged into a nightmare of double-speak, in which the military made speeches about morality as they tortured thousands and threw many of them alive from airplanes into the Rio de la Plata.

The estimated 30,000 disappeared have made Argentina infamous, and their absence testifies to a regime aiming to eliminate not just a guerrilla movement but also any vestige of independent thought in society. The clandestine torture camps and the theft of newborn babies from mothers killed after giving birth were no aberrations. They were part of a policy to radically alter the relations within society. They called it a 'Process of National Reorganisation' and that is indeed what they achieved. The effects were dramatic: generalised terror was fed by an information blackout and the ubiquitous military and police presence, and this fear broke down social relations. Individuals retreated into their families and close, trusted relationships while suspicion poisoned other encounters. The frightened blame-the-victim justifications of the time still haunt the country: 'they must have done something' (to deserve being taken by the military in the middle of the night never to be seen again), 'there must be a reason,' 'stay out of it...'

The silence of the era meant that any sign took on layers of meaning. Journalist Uki Goñi recalls a banner hung by the military on Buenos Aires' main avenue that read 'Silence is health'. Although it supposedly referred to drivers using their horns, the banner felt much more oppressive.

The murder by the state of a generation of people who believed in more equal social relations decimated the organisations which represented the least powerful in society. Trade unions, student organisations, progressive religious movements, any association of ordinary people from tenants' associations to school classrooms, all became a potential focus of subversion for the military.

Disciplining society: economics under the dictatorship

The balance of power between rulers and ruled was tipped decisively towards the military government and the economic establishment. The extreme level of violent control was necessary to carry out the economic changes the military put into motion: the massive transference of resources from the working class to the speculative oligarchy and the use of the state as banker of last resort for private interests. On March 24th 1977, the first anniversary of the coup, Rodolfo Walsh surfaced from clandestinity to post his Open Letter from a Writer to the Military Junta, an indictment which explodes the myth that nobody knew the extent of military actions even as everyone felt the terror. Walsh was already able to accuse the junta of specific crimes.

> 'Fifteen thousand disappeared, ten thousand prisoners, four thousand dead, hundreds of thousands uprooted; these are the raw statistics of terror. With normal prisons filled to overflowing, you created virtual concentration camps in the main barracks around the country, where no judge, lawyer, journalist or international observer ever sets foot.
>
> [...]
>
> 'These events, which stir the conscience of the civilised world, are not however the greatest suffering inflicted on the Argentinian people, nor the worst violation of human rights which you have

committed. It is in the economic policy of this government where one discovers not only the explanation of the crimes, but a greater atrocity which punishes millions of human beings through planned misery.'[10]

The same day, Walsh was gunned down on a street in Buenos Aires by a state 'task force', a death squad made up of senior military and police officers.

In 1974–75, salaries still made up 50 per cent of the country's wealth but by the beginning of 1977 they were only 32 per cent of the gross domestic product (GDP). The onslaught on trade unions was systematic and brutal. They were banned, but that was only the beginning. The military took control of and expanded the extra-judicial death squads which had been in action since the early 1970s and continued to murder and disappear labour leaders and their supporters, their lawyers and their relatives. At the same time, salaries were frozen in the face of inflation of up to 350 per cent,[11] a catastrophic loss of income for the majority of the population, who were paid in pesos and unable to afford hard currency.

The example of Chile was near in time and space, a dictatorship which imposed neo-liberal policies as the route to development. The Argentinian junta wasted no time in following Chile's example. The military's economy minister was José Martínez de Hoz, the scion of an oligarchic family. He was personally connected to a large number of national agro-industrial companies and foreign banks, among them the Chase Manhattan.

The main aims of the government's programme were to reduce the presence of the state in the economy while opening the economy to the international market. On assuming office, though, they had urgent work to do: inflation was high and reserves were low. They had only US$20 million, not enough to make payments due on the foreign debt. An agreement with the IMF was therefore of first necessity. Although the IMF had refused to negotiate with Isabelita's government, it immediately came to the aid of the new regime. A loan of US$100 million was enough to replenish the country's reserves and private banks came forward once again. A brief period of stability was achieved, with wages frozen, prices raised and optimism boosted by the influx of foreign investment that followed the IMF.

In practice, the goal of liberalising the economy meant making room for private capital, an effective privatisation of the state's regulatory role. One of Martínez de Hoz' first measures gives a sense of the interests he favoured: the state ceased to control the exports of cereals, ceding control to a handful of companies at the same time that the tax on agricultural exports was abolished. Thus one of the main wealth-generating activities in the country ceased to support the state and its profits became entirely private. The added factor of sending profits out of the country, a traditional practice of the landed oligarchy, meant a net transference of millions of dollars out of the economy. Unfortunately, the money was not immediately missed, as international credit was cheap and northern banks were falling over themselves to lend to poor countries.

At the same time, the main creation of the junta's economic policy was a financial market free of controls but subsidised in part by the state. The devastating effect of this contradiction would only become clear later. The way it worked in practice was that high interest rates and an overvalued peso meant that speculation became the most profitable economic activity. A speculator could invest dollars brought from abroad in short-term accounts with large profit margins, then take the earnings and the original capital out of the country freely. Meanwhile, industry was nowhere as profitable as speculation. Inflation was high, and reductions in tariffs encouraged cheap imports. Taken together, these factors led to a severe contraction of production and deindustrialisation. The theoretical aim of creating a market of capital to finance development had become an end in itself.

The icing on the cake was *'la tablita'*, a system in which changes in the official exchange rate were made according to a pre-announced schedule. *La tablita* was an attempt to bring down the overvalued peso, but it served mostly to give the free-moving capital a guarantee against which to place money in short term accounts – for a sure return.

The frenzy of short-term profiteering was unsustainable and in 1980 the financial system imploded. Inflation and interest rates hit all time highs, and the peso lost value as investors rushed to buy dollars and save themselves from the impending crash. In the process, banks began to go broke, and the state, liberal in name only, stepped in to guarantee deposits. It didn't stop the massive outflow of capital.

During the recession that began in 1978 and after banks began to go to the wall, the regime continued to allow total freedom to capital, in effect opening the door for capital flight on a scale never seen before. To sustain the financial system which encouraged the stampede, the state took on huge amounts of debt – US$8,000 million in 1980 alone – and used the reserves of the Central Bank to buttress failing private banks. Until Martínez de Hoz' removal from office halfway through 1981, US$5,400 million more was taken on in debt that year alone. The transference of resources from workers and industry to a financial market based on speculation and debt was underwritten by state borrowing reaching US$45,000 million by the end of the dictatorship in 1983, up from US$8,000 million in 1976, the year of the coup.

In 1981, the model broke down entirely. The drainage of deposits reached 25 per cent, the value of the peso plummeted and GDP contracted by 11.4 per cent (matched only by the nearly 10.9 per cent regression in 2002). Industrial production fell by 23 per cent, and the value of real wages by 20 per cent, wiping off purchasing power for the most vulnerable.

The events leading up to the crash of 1981 prefigured the crisis of 2001 in that the winners were the same: national capital which speculated and amassed fortunes was given enough time by the state to make sure its money was safely abroad by the time the crash came. Even worse, the debts contracted by private business were taken on by the state. The military changed the constitution so that the nation could take responsibility for private losses, leading to the creation of a debt burden that became a dead weight on the country. Thus, the government that claimed it would take the state out of the economy, and whose liberal credentials seemed as old as the oligarchy which supported it, financed a capital market where private companies and individuals made a fortune and the impoverished citizens of the state were left owing one.

The declared priority of the economic team had been to combat inflation, yet price increases ran at between 90 and 170 per cent in the years 1976 to 1980. Clearly for those with enough foreign currency for the peso to be a gambling chit, inflation was not a problem. When the government fixed the exchange rate and the rich had dollars, inflation rather suited them. There are questions as to whether it was planned that way, but certainly the results of economic policy during the dictatorship were in keeping with its overall aims: to weaken the working and middle classes and reinforce the power of a small economic elite.

The ultimate economic results of the dictatorship were to break workers' power, to transfer millions of dollars from the (salaried) taxpayer to the speculative oligarchy and foreign investors, and finally, to ensure that the indebtedness of private concerns in their orgy of speculative profit-making was taken on by the state. The national and international interests which used the financial markets to make spectacular short-term profits learnt it was possible to ransack a country and walk away with impunity. This lesson was too attractive to forget, while the victims of the robbery didn't know what had hit them. It was a dirty economic war that went hand-in-hand with the illegal war waged by the military on society. The final results (and aims) of the policies imposed were to privatise gains and socialise losses.

As the 'Process' began to unravel and internal differences showed up between the forces and factions in the military, the junta had to be seen to manage the economy better. Martínez de Hoz was replaced in 1981, although his economic vision lived on. By losing the Malvinas/Falklands war in 1982, the military squandered what little credibility they had after managing the economy against the poor and carrying out an ideological war against civilians. They were defeated but unbowed, and left the country economically and morally bankrupt.

Debt upon debt

The early 2002 devaluation brought tourists to the country in droves. They struggled to spend much even as they ate grandly, learnt to dance tango, flew to glaciers and jungles, picked up leather bargains and visited new museums in Buenos Aires, like the ambitious Museum of Latin American Art (MALBA). Soon they'll be able to visit the new Museum of Foreign Debt. Or maybe they'll pass.

The debt museum is an initiative of the Department of Economic Sciences at the University of Buenos Aires. Researchers are working to create a documentation centre to provide a teaching tool on the history of public debt in Argentina.

Argentina's recent problems underline that the 'debt crisis' which was associated with developing countries in the 1980s has not gone away. Debt is a reality of all national economies and needn't be a critical factor. The United States owes over US$6 trillion dollars, but as the economic and military world superpower, it can offer unparalleled collateral. Debt becomes a problem when the ways of generating wealth, or access to credit, are in question. As with personal debts, the affluent can get cheap credit while the poor get loan sharks – it's about money, but it is mostly about power.

Argentina has had long experience of the risks inherent to debt-driven capitalist expansion. An intense boom of speculation and export-led growth in Argentina went bust in 1890 when the country owed Barings Bank 21 million pounds which it could not fully repay. The Barings were rescued by the British government and the City of London financiers. Debt crises in the future would share another characteristic with that historic breaking of the Barings Bank: Argentina would pay the amount lent many times over in spite of defaulting, as the inherent risk was punished with high interest rates and parts of the loan 'held back' against repayment. Debt only happens when another is willing to lend, and money lending is not a charitable endeavour. There were always bankers ready to give credit to Argentina because the returns were handsome.

History has shown that countries that have repaid their foreign debt are the exception rather than the rule. As long ago as 1924, John Maynard Keynes wrote that the foreign governments that had defaulted on their external debt were so numerous, so nearly universal, that it was easier to point out those that had not defaulted than those who had.[12]

There is a myth in Argentina that the years of the rise and establishment of Perón and his support for workers' organisation were a time of reckless spending and irresponsible largesse to the working class – this judgement clearly coming from elite interests and not from the workers. In reality, social and economic changes were achieved with national resources, while external debt was reduced.[13] In 1913 almost half of the capital invested in the country was foreign, yet that proportion dropped to 20 per cent by 1940, 15 per cent in 1945 and five per cent between 1949 and 1955. These figures show that foreign investment is not as necessary to development as neo-liberals would claim.

Argentina has been a creditor, too. After World War II, Britain owed a great deal for the meat and grain supplied to it during the war. Britain's attitude at the time is enlightening: it refused to pay, claiming it was unable to. Instead it offered payment in kind and forced buying of expensive British goods

– hence the railway expansion after 1946.[14] Inability to pay is not an argument rich countries countenance from poor ones, even from those which clearly lack even basic necessities (Haiti, Nicaragua, most countries of Africa … the list is long.).

In Argentina debts were taken and paid back in the 1950s and up until the 1970s, but amounts were not significant enough to impact strongly on the economic life of the country. Military governments from 1966 to 1973 increased public debt to international creditors to US$3,782 million, while private companies took out about the same amount. During the brief return of Perón between 1973 and 1974 no new debts were agreed.

The recent history of Argentina as a country in hock began after 1976. Argentina in the twenty-first century is suffering the hangover of a few years of gambling when the rich earned fabulous sums because they had rigged the game, and to top it all, they made the state responsible for picking up the losses when the game was up. The gambler had a few variants to choose from. One went like this: the economy minister, Martínez de Hoz, decided to liberalise financial transactions so that money could be brought in and be taken out of the country at will. The high interest rates succeeded in attracting capital, but only to short-term deposits.

The gap between rich and poor grew as the former kept the value of their money by buying dollars instead of holding pesos, while the latter only had pesos, which lost their value daily. Demand for foreign currency was so high that the state forced public companies to take out 'phantom' credits in order to make dollars available to private investors. They in turn bought the dollars, took them out of the country for safekeeping, and used that as collateral to get more loans to buy more currency to 'invest' in Argentina, profit on the high interest rate and then take the proceeds out again. It was called the 'financial bicycle', one of a range of get-rich-quick schemes of which everybody tried to partake.

Illegal Debt

Campaigner Alejandro Olmos is a social activist who had fought oppression from within the ranks of Peronism since the 1950s. He took his conviction that Argentina's debt was illegitimate to court, and won. Here he explains his legal success.

'We have, our friends, the sad privilege of having carried out a penal investigation about external debt [in Argentina], a debt which amounts to the greatest swindle ever suffered by Argentinians. Since 1982, and still during the dictatorship run by the Military Junta, I have been taking forward a judicial investigation which has brought together the evidence of this fraud. I bring a vision which escapes the technocrats, because the Argentinian external debt is the result of a gigantic dominance through procedures punishable by the legal code. The judicial investigators who carried out a thorough investigation into the institutions of the state found that the actions which generated debts constituted illegal acts. And clearly, if the debt was generated through delinquent forms of economic planning, it cannot be legitimate. This vision of debt is not whimsical or partial, but comes out of a voluminous judicial process in which legal assessments were fundamental parts of the evidence presented, and those experts are not allowed ideological biases. They included an ad-hoc Commission named by the Federal Tribunal and made up of experts proposed by the National Academy of Economic Sciences, the Economic Science Faculty and the Committee of Professional Economists, among other judicial experts, who together researched the role of the Central Bank and state companies. Among these last, I would highlight, as an example of ignominy, YPF, the national oil company, among the largest in Latin America. Experts determined that YPF appeared to have contracted debts of US$6,000 million, but in fact not a single dollar had entered their books. State companies were used as 'fronts' for external debt agreements. And the cash remained in the Central Bank. The explanation given to the Tribunal by those responsible at the time was that the cash was used to "open up the economy".'

One result of the furious pedalling was that by the end of the dictatorship, for every dollar owed by the state, there was at least one dollar owned by an Argentinian and deposited in a foreign bank account. This was perhaps the most important dynamic established by the dictatorship, one that would continue after the return of democracy. The logic culminated in the profits made by buying cut-price privatised companies with Argentinian capital held abroad in the 1990s and selling them on for their real worth and the profits taken out of the country again.

By the time the military withdrew from power in 1983, Argentinians owed US$43,000 million. Economist Eric Calcagno calculated that the debts contracted during the 'years of lead' broke down roughly into 44 per cent in financing the export or flight of capital by private national and international interests; 33 per cent in financing the debts taken out; and 23 per cent in buying armament and other undeclared imports.[15]

The legacy of debt poisoned the democratic period which began in 1983. The weight of the debt caught the first civilian government between the rock of the IMF and creditors' demands and the hard place of having to squeeze a population impoverished by inflation to pay the debt. The result was compromise and chaos fanned by inflation into a social conflagration, as we shall see below. Even worse, servicing the debt meant contracting new debts, so that even as repayments choked the economy, the debt got bigger. The unsustainable amounts of debt inherited by civilian rule in 1983 contributed to the failures of the first democratic government.

The second civilian government was headed by Carlos Menem. For the first two years, there seemed to be no way to balance the books – until US Treasury Secretary Nicholas Brady came up with a solution for the creditors. As the 1982 debt crisis sparked by Mexico's default dragged on, it became clear that developing countries were not going to see economic recoveries strong enough to pay the high interest that had accumulated. The Brady Plan required economic reform in line with creditors' ideas of sound financial management, and allowed for debt to be turned into bonds to be sold, both diversifying the debt owed and pushing payment into the future. In 1992 Argentina signed up to it.

In spite of these financial dealings, Menem's two stints in office (1989–1999) managed to double the debt load. In December 1991, the neo-liberal course was set as the exchange rate was fixed at one dollar for one peso. At that point, external debt amounted to US$61,337 million. A decade later, as the model crashed, debt had grown to a monstrous US$140,190 million.

As campaigners against third world debt, Jubilee Plus,[16] put it:

> 'Argentina's crisis illuminates an unpalatable truth about globalisation: it is the evolution of capitalism into a system of dominance by the few; those who have access to, and control over finance capital; but who are not accountable either to the market, to the rule of law or to democratic institutions.'[17]

By 2001 the 'future' had arrived and even the re-structured debts were due with their double digit high risk interest. The attempts to put off the day of reckoning failed with the notorious default declared by Argentina's seven-day President Adolfo Rodríguez Saá on December 23rd 2001. A better mechanism to keep developing countries subject to rich countries' pressure could not have been dreamed up.

Return to democracy in 1983

The military made way for civilian elections and in 1983 a new government led by the Radicals was democratically elected. The party that had lifted the middle classes into power at the beginning of the twentieth century had a revival. Raúl Alfonsín, their leader, campaigned on promises of justice for the crimes of the last dictatorship and the return of the rule of law. For the first time in its history, Peronism lost fair elections. The 1980s were its years in the wilderness, when the movement sought to re-establish itself at national level.

The flag of human rights waved by Alfonsín was unfurled in a social context of hope and relief. Once in power, his priorities were to improve the newly-acquired democracy and its frail institutions, using a strong ethical discourse and a reliance on broad public support. He set out publicly his aim of bringing private or sectoral interests under the control of the state, and most important of these, he promised to subject the military to civilian rule.

In the first two years of government it seemed his promises could be fulfilled. His government set up the Comisión Nacional sobre la Desaparación de Personas, CONADEP (National Commission on the Disappearance of People), which documented the atrocities carried out by the military dictatorship. The final report, published as *Nunca Más* (Never Again), was a bestseller, as the society that had preferred not to know came to accept the enormity of what had happened.

Human rights groups initiated lawsuits against the repressors and initially the Alfonsín government sought to have the military admit their errors and carry out their own purge. Alfonsín encouraged prosecutors to limit themselves to the intellectual authors of the 'Process' and to let off lower-ranking officers under the premise that they were 'only following orders'. They refused to do anything of the sort and military courts threw out the cases against the leaders of the juntas.

The attempts to achieve justice were met with the still-strong power of the military, but the public pressure against impunity was running high. Supported by that public pressure, a provincial judiciary made a courageous show of autonomy that led to the use of civil law to bring the junta members to trial. The world watched as the nine junta leaders were eventually tried in civilian courts. Five were found guilty of gross violations of human rights and went to jail, an unprecedented, if partial, success.

Arguing the need to preserve democracy and avert a military

coup, Alfonsín and the Radicals passed two laws soon after the trials. In 1986, the law of *Punto Final* (Full Stop) to put a time limit on legal proceedings, and in 1987, *Obediencia Debida* (Due Obedience) let off lower-ranking officers. No other party in Congress supported these laws. The right and Peronism wanted a full amnesty, while the left wanted nothing to do with capitulating to the military. Alfonsín's attempt at a political accommodation infuriated human rights groups, bringing on a flood of judicial cases to fit within the two-month timeframe allowed by Punto Final. Alfonsín's political response had been negotiated in the corridors of power, and left the majority of the population, who rejected impunity, out of the picture.

As the cases that had been lodged continued to go through the courts, a faction of the military staged an uprising during Easter 1987. Colonel Aldo Rico and a group of middle-ranking officers took a military base and demanded both an end to the trials against the military and a recognition of their patriotic conduct during the dictatorship. Although they did not represent the forces at large, there was general agreement with their demands among the ranks and no other part of the army was willing to put them down by force. Society's response was overwhelming, though: repudiation was heard from all quarters and people took to the streets in the millions, holding vigils in streets and public squares during the four days of the uprising.

The message could not have been clearer: there was no support for military rule and people were willing to defend democracy with their lives. The crisis ended when Alfonsín went in person to negotiate with the rebels, but his standing was damaged, not so much by what transpired there, but by the impression it gave. He agreed that the government would support the laws already passed, and the officers took responsibility for the uprising. Legally and institutionally, nothing had changed, but there was a widespread sense in society that Argentina's shiny new democracy had been tarnished and that Alfonsín had capitulated when confronted by the military, which was therefore not under civilian control at all.

Alfonsín began to lose the authority to steer the country when he failed to overpower the military. And the population's disappointment with him and with democracy, increasingly coloured the perceptions of his ability to fix the economy. In fact, on the economic front nothing was going right. The financial legacy of the dictatorship kept the country in crisis. It both ravaged productivity and deepened dependency on international loans to deal with the inherited debt. Inflation became structural, tax evasion grew and since nobody had faith in the peso, everyone sought to have dollars instead. Although Alfonsín initially rejected offers of 'help' from the IMF, after a year he found himself having to use IMF loans to meet debt repayments. And so the government tried to impose some of the adjustment measures required by the loans and some of them brought stability for a short while. One reason why the measures were only half-hearted was the need to maintain the support of society, which required protecting people from the costs of severe adjustment. Alfonsín was losing on all sides. The re-structuring was never enough for the IMF, although they did disburse money as their conditions were reluctantly taken on. And the people did pay, suffering the recession brought on by austerity and the inflation which emerged every time the bottom line did not add up.

The inherited problems were not overcome and by 1985 inflation was running at 5,000 per cent. Although inflation had been high enough to create anxiety for a decade, it was now officially 'hyper', accelerating the fall to poverty for many. In 1985 the government launched the Plan Austral with a new currency, the *austral,* and a range of measures to curb state expenditure, begin privatisation and boost exports. The package worked well for two years, and then the slide towards inflation began again. In 1988 Alfonsín defaulted on the external debt, as reserves were insufficient to meet payments due and the country once more faced crisis.

Fear of Inflation

Inflation is *the* economic bogeyman in Europe and the Americas. From the infamous Tory claim in the UK in the 1980s that unemployment was the price worth paying for low inflation, to the desperate measures taken in Latin America also in the 1980s to combat three-digit inflation figures, the fear that money would rapidly lose its value has often taken precedence over any other economic indicator – and was decisive in Argentina agreeing to take the neo-liberal medicine.

The frequency with which inflation is mentioned in a history of Argentina points to the central role it has played in the political and social life of the country. Economist Héctor García reflects that 'currency is a social exchange based on trust' and the inability of Argentina to sustain a stable currency probably bears some relation to the levels of mistrust and conflict in society between economic interests and classes. If one believes that the economy is the basis for social relations, we can see that inflation itself contributes to a spiral of economic violence that undermines trust.

Inflation also hits the poor hardest. Their income is the not only the lowest, but the most likely to be fixed. 'Basic needs' make up a much higher proportion of their expenditure, so when the cost of food and services rises suddenly, their income is not enough to cover the basics. On top of that, hikes in the price of basic goods tend to outpace the general rate of inflation.

Argentina has suffered recurring bouts of inflation – and they are indelibly etched in people's memories as moments of intense anxiety and uncertainty. For all but the best-off sectors of society, inflation meant months, sometimes years of not knowing whether a salary could stretch to buy food at the end of the month.

Osvaldo Soriano, one of Argentina's best-loved authors, wrote this about living with inflation:

'In Buenos Aires in 1985, it was no longer possible to buy anything at night for what it had cost in the morning. In the cafés, the cashiers went crazy between the orders of clients and the demands of the boss, who spent his time listening to the escalation of prices on the radio. [...] Wallets were not a good present for anyone. There was no room in their compartments to keep paper with the value of 100,000, of 500,000, of 1,000,000 pesos.'[18]

The last episode of hyperinflation in 1989 served as the trauma that pushed desperate Argentinians to sign up to neo-liberalism and parity with the dollar. In 1989 inflation came close to 5,000 per cent in the year, and in 1990 was still running at 1,300 per cent. It came down to double figures in 1991 and 1992, but it wasn't until 1993 that it came down to single figures after the Convertibility Law required the Central Bank to have a dollar for each peso issued.

In 1989, Peronist Carlos Menem won the presidential election. By then the economic situation had become untenable. The austral had lost forty times its value in the course of the year. Monthly inflation ran as high as 200 per cent, and the year's total was the worst the country had ever seen. Salaries became worthless by pay day, and savings lost the accumulated value of years in hours. Menem won because any change seemed better than the crisis they were living through, in which the daily battle for survival absorbed all energy and the future ceased to exist. The ransacking of supermarkets and food riots made Alfonsín's position untenable and he made an ignominious exit from power five months before he was due to leave the Casa Rosada, leaving chaos behind him.

Notes

1   Thorp, R. 1998, *Progress, poverty and exclusion: an economic history of Latin America in the 20th century*, Baltimore, Johns Hopkins University Press for the Inter-American Development Bank, p.50

2   Hunt, L. 1996, *Barings lost: Nick Leeson and the collapse of Barings Plc*, New York, Butterworth-Heinemann

3   Between 1820 and 1930 (primarily 1860–1914), 62 million people emigrated to the Americas from Europe and Asia. Of those, 61 per cent went to the United States and 12 per cent to Canada, but Argentina and Brazil came next with ten and seven per cent respectively. Thorp, op cit. p.49

4   For comparative work see, for example, D.C.M. Platts and Guido di Tella (Eds.) *Argentina, Australia and Canada: studies in comparative development 1870-1965*, London, MacMillan, 1985

5   Op cit. Thorp, p.65

6   James, D. 1988, *Resistance and integration: Peronism and the Argentine working class, 1946–1976*, Cambridge, Cambridge University Press

7   INDEC, http://www.indec.mecon.ar/

8   Jozami, A. 2003, *Argentina: la destrucción de una nación*, Buenos Aires, Mondadori, p.287

9   Tosco, Agustín 1984, *Presente en las luchas de la clase obrera*, Argentina, Editorial Lanot

10 McCaughan, M. 2002, *True crimes, Rodolfo Walsh, the life and times of a radical intellectual*, London, Latin America Bureau

11 Jozami, op cit.

12 Calcagno, A.E and E. Calcagno 2002, *La deuda externa explicada a todos (los que tienen que pagarla)*, Buenos Aires, Catálogos, p.94 quoting John Maynard Keynes, 'Defaults by foreign governments' from *The collected writings of John Maynard Keynes*, Vol. XVIII 1922–1932 Macmillan, Cambridge, 1978

13 Ibid. p.38

14 Ibid.

15 Ibid. p.49

16 The successor to Jubilee 2000, a worldwide movement to abolish unsustainable debt for poor countries.
    See http://www.jubilee2000uk.org/

17 Pettifor, A., L. Cisneros and A. Olmos Gaona 'Creditor co-responsibility for Argentina's crisis – and the need for independent resolution,' Jubilee Plus Report, September 2001
    http://www.jubilee2000uk.org/analysis/reports/tango_exec.htm

18 In Nouzeilles, G. and G. Montaldo (Eds.) 2002, *The Argentina Reader*, Durham, Duke University Press, p.482

3
Risk and Responsibility

'…the largest financial collapse of any country in history…'
New York Times, November 3 2001

One peso, one dollar?

Once Menem assumed power, he made both a 'U' turn from his populist campaign promises and a decisive break with Peronist tradition. Menem became the ready heir of Martínez de Hoz, finishing the liberalisation project that had first given Argentina the loss of industry and an unpayable external debt. In the 1990s both debt and deindustrialisation were brought to extremes through a liberalisation carried out with no checks or transparency. The dictatorship broke organised labour, the dream of the oligarchy since Peronism had first appeared. Menem co-opted organised labour and broke individual workers through unemployment and the price increases that came with stability.

His first economic measure was to invite a senior executive of the Argentinian transnational company Bunge and Born to be economy minister. Bunge and Born is the largest company in the country, and part of the staunchly conservative oligarchic establishment. The appointment of two successive company representatives to the ministry was the first example of the magical thinking Menem applied to economic policy throughout his tenure. The idea was that a successful company should be able to steer the country to wealth, as it does for its own shareholders. It didn't work, perhaps because national enterprise was too used to making its profits by exploiting the state via subsidies, tax exemptions and speculation.

For the first 18 months of Menem's mandate none of his three successive economy ministers succeeded in using the adjustment policies they implemented to actually stop inflation and activate the economy. In 1990, high-profile journalist Horacio Verbitsky could see the scale of the disaster that was coming. In his book *La Educación Presidencial* (Educating the President) he notes that, 'a thousand industrial workers have been sacked and three thousand suspended every day in March [1990], defining a catastrophe without precedent in recent Argentinian history. After a gathering to support Menem in April, he responded thus to the greatest question worrying anyone interested in social pathology: "The Argentinian people are going to suffer a lot more."'

Enter, stage right, Domingo Cavallo and his financial incantations. While minister for foreign affairs (1989–1991), he dreamt up the Plan Bonex, whereby the state effectively stole the savings of some 200,000 people, most of them small-scale savers. The plan involved confiscating US$4,600 million and turning them into bonds – a certificate which is evidence of a debt on which the issuer promises to pay the holder a specified amount of interest for a specified length of time, and to repay the loan on its maturity. The bonds traded at only a quarter of their value at first, meaning that savers who had to cash their bonds lost most of their money. This move saved the banking system from collapse, but the economy continued to deteriorate. By 1991 the country was facing its third inflation crisis in two years and Menem's future seemed uncertain.

Domingo Cavallo

A Catholic and conservative native of the province of Córdoba, Cavallo graduated in economics and went on to Harvard University in the United States. He was a young and recent doctoral graduate when he became an official in the Interior Ministry during the dictatorship, in 1976.   ‖▶

He is better known for having been appointed head of the Central Bank in 1982, towards the end of the military government. There he earned the gratitude of the richest speculators by further developing the mechanism through which the state (and the taxpayer) assumed the debt of private companies and individuals. He guaranteed impunity for the economic terrorists who operated under cover of the state terrorism of the junta.

He dedicated the 1980s to creating a think-tank and lobby platform for wealthy liberals, but by 1987 he was back in politics in the surprising company of the Peronists, historically his ideological opposites. It was a good indication of the direction in which Menem was to take Perón's Partido Justicialista.

He was economy minister between 1991 and 1995, implementing the Convertibility Plan and negotiating Argentina's entry into the Brady Plan. The latter involved the emission of government bonds on a grand scale and made external debt the mechanism through which state assets could be bought on the cheap.

In 1995 Cavallo resigned after losing Menem's support when he sought to expose corruption surrounding the privatisation of the postal service. In 1997 he founded his own right-wing political party, Acción por la República (Action for the Republic). In 2001, floundering President de la Rúa used him as a last resort to inspire confidence in creditors, appointing him economy minister once more. But his black magic ceased to work even as he suggested ever-grander bond scams. His last legacy was the corralito. Much of the fury unleashed on December 19th and 20th 2001 was directed at him and when he resigned in the small hours of the 20th, he requested extra security for himself and his family.

In 2003 he lived in New York City and taught at Columbia University. He has been accused of complicity in arms dealing to Ecuador and Croatia in the same investigations that involve ex-President Menem, and faces the possibility of time behind bars – unlike his fortune, of unknown value, nowhere to be found inside the corralón.

In 1991 Cavallo unveiled his plan to stop inflation once and for all. The answer was the Law of Convertibility, which tightened monetary policy much as aging beauties were having their skin stretched. One peso was decreed to be the same value as one dollar, and that was the mantra of the 1990s. Devaluation became illegal. The Central Bank had to possess a dollar for every peso it printed and that would solve all the nation's problems. It seemed like magic, and it was. The trick was hidden up the sleeves of the politicians and capitalist owners and involved selling much of what the state owned, reducing state obligations and borrowing a fortune. The con lay in the illusion that convertibility could be sustained by borrowing and foreign investment. It couldn't.

But for a short time in the early 1990s investment figures were dizzying. A combination of international growth and the return of a significant part of Argentinian capital held abroad meant vast sums were made available to buy up privatisation bargains. But as they were sold on, the money returned to its foreign havens. *Le Monde Diplomatique* in Argentina carried the view that 'the fixed exchange rate makes us extremely dependent on a large volume of external capital, and so convertibility brings up, in truth, the dilemma of dependence or sovereignty, of what kind of country we want.'[1]

The kind of country everyone wanted was the same as the dreams of glory since the export heyday of the early twentieth century: a rich nation among the most developed in the world. The worth of the peso made foreign goods affordable and fed the belief that Argentina was finally on the way to long-term prosperity. Macro-economic growth figures were among the best in the world in the early 1990s, and socially it translated into the hope that the unstable past was firmly left behind. For the middle classes there was consumption, travel and the chance to buy Amazon books online from the US and get them delivered by the newly-privatised postal service. For those in work, stability meant credit and the intoxicating feeling of being able to afford conspicuous consumption. In the UK a 25-year mortgage at low interest rates is taken for granted; in Argentina it had always been as distant as a dream. Then in the 1990s it became possible, although interest rates were considerably higher than those in Europe. Advanced capitalism had arrived.

Even the poor wanted to believe that wealth would trickle down. As Alicia Unzalú, of the Centro Ecuménico de Educación Popular (Ecumenical Popular Education Centre) in Buenos Aires, says, 'December 2001 was a major turning point. Before that, many people believed Menem's talk of Argentina joining the First World. The middle classes thought their four-wheel drives and country clubs were forever. As long as they had work, ordinary working class people felt part of the system – they expected to send their kids to school, and one day to be able to buy a house. Now that certainty has gone.'[2]

President Menem sold convertibility to the country as the only way to control the dreaded hyperinflation that had destroyed the previous government and undermined the rule of the dictators a decade previous. The costs were hidden, and for the length of the 1990s, the population preferred to ignore them. The mantra of one peso, one dollar was considered the reassuring sign that Argentina was OK – hence the reluctance to ditch the measure in the late 1990s, when it was asphyxiating the economy.

The losers were those out of work, whose jobs had been 'rationalised' through privatisation and the flood of cheap imports that closed down many industrial and manufacturing enterprises. The victims of these closures became the mass of unemployed who by 2001 reached over 20 per cent of the economically active population, while under-employment accounted for another 20-plus per cent. Even during the worst of hyperinflation, unemployment had not gone beyond single figures, hovering around six per cent during the 1980s. But in 1993 it stood at ten per cent and during the decade the figure rose inexorably to reach the untenable levels of 2001.

And the drastic measures undertaken to control inflation had side effects: in the first months of the Convertibility Plan in 1991, prices rose by almost 60 per cent, while salaries were frozen.

In the end, it wasn't the internal contradiction that pushed Argentina to devalue, but external factors.

In the late 1990s, a number of Asian economies went into crisis, and the shock waves were felt around the world. By 1999 the effects had reached Brazil, with its own currency, the *real*, pegged to the dollar. The Brazilian government spent a fortune trying to back the real, but eventually gave up and allowed it to float freely (and promptly lose value), allowing for exports to regain competitiveness. Brazil is Argentina's main trading partner, and the overvalued peso became very expensive in the newly-devalued Brazil. That, economic pundits agree, was the time when Argentina should have devalued the peso. But it wasn't only illegal, it was also unthinkable.

For most people the mantra of one peso, one dollar had little to do with esoteric currency fluctuations. The fixed exchange rate came to stand for stability and credit and 'having made it'. And so no politician could seriously suggest abandoning it, even as commentators agreed its collapse was inevitable.

Joseph Stiglitz, former economist at the World Bank and Nobel Prize winner, sums up the problems Argentina brought on itself by pegging the peso to the dollar:

'Had most of Argentina's trade been with the United States, pegging the peso to the dollar might have made sense. But much of Argentina's trade was with Europe and Brazil. The strong (most would say, overvalued) dollar has meant enormous American trade deficits. But with the Argentine peso pegged to the dollar, an overvalued dollar means an overvalued peso. And while the United States has been able to sustain trade deficits, Argentina could not. Whenever you have a massive trade deficit, you have to borrow from abroad to finance it. Although the United States is now the world's largest debtor country, outsiders are still willing to lend us money. They were willing to lend to Argentina, too, when it had the IMF stamp of approval.'[3]

When Argentina lost the confidence of the IMF, its unwillingness to lend any more couldn't have been more decisive. In December 2001 it refused to disburse an already-agreed loan, triggering the colossal default. Up until then, it had provided enough time and money for banks to take US$15,000 million out of the country during 2001; by November it decided that it could pull the plug, as the losers from a major default would only include the Argentinian people and some European banks. With no fresh money to pay debts, the country was forced to default on about US$95,000 million of the US$141,000 million foreign debt – and the country plunged into crisis.

Even Domingo Cavallo, who had been on excellent terms with the Fund, admitted that the IMF 'seems to want to hurt Argentina with their intransigence,' when they refused to transfer the foreseen US$1,260 million. It was part of a package negotiated in 2000 to secure the banking system, which did just that, at the cost of ignoring the fundamentals of the economy, which were heading steadily toward meltdown.[4] The IMF refusal might have made sense if the Fund had been critical of the policies which had led Argentina to the situation it found itself in. But Argentina had been consistently portrayed by the US and the IMF as the best example of neo-liberal policies.

Multiple international failures: the role of the IMF

The organisation created at Bretton Woods after World War II to help countries in financial trouble has 'FMI' as its Spanish acronym. An Argentinian journalist, Alfredo Zaiat of *Página/12*, has renamed it after its recent actions *Fracasos Múltiples Internacionales*, Multiple International Failures.

The long list of crises triggered by IMF-imposed conditions in developing country economies raises the suspicion that they can't be entirely accidental. One economic meltdown might be forgivable, two rather careless, but the string of social and economic disasters while the IMF was chief economic advisor suggests that there is a logic to this consistent undermining of developing economies.

The IMF's mission is simple. According to itself, it is 'an international organization of 184 member countries. It was established to promote international monetary cooperation, exchange stability, and orderly exchange arrangements; to foster economic growth and high levels of employment; and to provide temporary financial assistance to countries to help ease balance of payments adjustment.'[5]

All that sounds like a good idea, but the reality is rather different. What should be 'orderly exchange' has become more like debt collection for rich countries, and as to fostering 'economic growth and high levels of employment,' the IMF does exactly the opposite. It does provide temporary financial assistance to help with balance of payments, that is, loans that allow countries to pay their debts in hard currency to northern governments and banks.

The IMF is supposed to be a mutual aid society where economies are strengthened. Instead, it has often appeared an instrument of US policy, practically indistinguishable from the Treasury Department. In 2003, Argentina's crisis woke up European countries and Japan to the use of the IMF to further their interests. For all the rich countries, fulfilling international obligations like debt payments takes precedence over the welfare and development of nations – something known to be counterproductive at least since reparations were extracted from Germany after World War I.

And unlike other international bodies such as the United Nations, votes are determined by contribution levels, so that IMF member countries do not have equality even in name. Countries pay to be members, and Argentina has to pay around US$1,200 million a year for the privilege. The US government has by far the greatest influence with 18 per cent of the voting shares in

> ## Greg Palast interviews former World Bank economist and Nobel Prize winner Joseph Stiglitz
>
> The four steps of IMF policy according to Joseph Stiglitz:
>
> 'Step One, privatization – which Stiglitz said could more accurately be called, "briberization". Step Two of the IMF/World Bank one-size-fits-all rescue-your-economy plan is "Capital Market Liberalization". Stiglitz calls this the "Hot Money" cycle. Cash comes in for speculation in real estate and currency, then flees at the first whiff of trouble. Step Three, "Market-Based Pricing", a fancy term for raising prices on food, water and cooking gas. This leads, predictably, to Step-Three-and-a-Half: what Stiglitz calls "The IMF riot." Step Four of what the IMF and World Bank call their "poverty reduction strategy": Free Trade. This is free trade by the rules of the World Trade Organization and World Bank. Stiglitz, the insider, likens free trade WTO-style to the Opium Wars. "That too was about opening markets," he said. 'It's a little like the Middle Ages," [he] told me, "When the patient died they would say, 'well, he stopped the bloodletting too soon, he still had a little blood in him'".'[6]

the Fund, which gives it de facto control. Over the years, the IMF has been active as a branch of US foreign policy, creating the best international conditions for US economic interests.

Since the developing world debt crisis of the 1980s, the IMF has become the leader of the creditors' cartel. Its importance resides in the fact that a 'nay' from the Fund can mean a country gets no credit from anywhere and becomes an economic pariah state. Few countries have seriously called its bluff.

The same set of IMF conditions for poor countries is endlessly repeated: opening capital markets, privatisation, reduction in state spending, boosting exports. Who benefits from these measures? Privatisation means international interests can buy up new ventures. Less state expenditure means more unemployment and cheaper labour. Boosting exports means more dollar to pay debts while cheap raw materials are abundant on the world market.

The main beneficiaries are clearly not meant to be the inhabitants of the country being subjected to these measures. Meanwhile, debt balloons due to interest rate hikes decided in rich countries and result in the original loan being repaid many times over.

These have been the IMF blanket remedies for decades, but before the 1980s the Fund did not have the leverage of external debt. The military dictatorship that ousted Perón arranged for Argentina to join the IMF and the World Bank in 1956. Already in 1958 a weak civilian president sandwiched between military dictatorships signed the first agreement with the Fund, a 'plan for stabilisation and development.' Before 'neo' there was already liberalism, and the IMF recipe included the now well-known recipe of reduction in state expenditure, privatisation of public enterprises, hikes in service charges and freezing of wages. As ever, such severe attacks on people's livelihoods had to be backed up with repressive force. Workers' protests were put down by the army, while the country lived under generalised repression that included the banning of Peronism.

The IMF went on to happily finance the dictatorship's liberalisation programme, undeterred by the violence with which it was being implemented. In the 1980s, the Fund finally succeeded in convincing President Alfonsín that it had the solution to the volatile economic situation, and through the classic means of structural adjustment achieved short-term stability and long-term recession.

During the 1990s Argentina was the 'good example' the IMF liked to boast about. Inflation was down, foreign investment was up, and privatisation was ubiquitous. President Menem was invited to address the Board of Governors of the IMF and the World Bank to show off the star pupil. His speech on

Argentina's fiscal rectitude and spending sobriety was supposed to prove that structural adjustment wasn't only good for the rich nations, but helped the poorer country too.[7] He claimed to have achieved 'an absolute economic miracle'. He didn't mention the social costs or explain that the radical measures were cautiously accepted by a population exhausted by hyper-inflation and insecurity. Argentines wanted stability at any price, but they had not bargained for the size of the bill. They only became aware of its magnitude in December 2001.

According to the IMF itself, it sent some 50 missions to Argentina between 1991 and 2002 to look into fiscal, monetary and banking matters. And the praise kept coming as long as public expenditure was curtailed. Beware those who bring ful-some praise, as Atilio Borón, a sociologist who heads the Latin American Council of Social Sciences (CLACSO) underlines:

'The admirers are the world financial establishments, the Director General of the IMF, the President of the World Bank, the Secretary of the United States Treasury, the White House, the leaders of G-7, the international financial press, the large financial speculators, the CEOs of the monopoly conglomerates, etc. [...] they said of Menem that he was a valiant governor, that he had abandoned his far flown ideas characterised by populism and state intervention, that he demonstrated prudence and good sense in the management of the public budget, that he had learnt to interpret market signals correctly, that he had overcome the irrational populist fear of globalisation. They also praised his "reformist" zeal in social security matters, in the opening of the markets, in financial deregulation and in the privatisation of state-owned companies. His calls to "modernise" the trade unions and to "de-ideologise" labour negotiations were received with a round of applause...

'These people and their immense propaganda apparatus repeated every day that Argentina was on the right track, was a model to imitate, that its future was secure and many other lies of the kind. When the debacle occurred all these individuals fell silent and blamed the Argentines for the disaster.'[8]

Even as the implosion of the economy and representative politics was generating daily confrontations in 2001, the IMF was busy telling Argentinians that they had to sort the crisis out themselves, and they would only receive help if they agreed to certain conditions. Among them was the revocation of the law of 'Economic Subversion' (first created in 1974 and altered ten years later). This annulment would ensure that any financial damage inflicted on the state by the banks, and the financial sector, would enjoy complete impunity.

The Fund claimed that the law, which sanctioned crimes against the national economy, violated investors' judicial security because it was too vague and far-reaching. It seemed no coincidence that the IMF forced Argentina to repeal the law in the aftermath of massive capital flight planned and executed by the financial sector and other international interests. In May 2002 Congress duly revoked the law, paving the way for an 'agreement' with the IMF.

In case there were any doubt as to the intentions of the IMF (in protecting those who have committed crimes, if nothing else), its pressure in relation to the corralón (the freezing of bank accounts) is instructive. First the IMF criticised this policy as an affront to private property and therefore the rule of law. Yet when it came to legal rulings that might have forced banks to return deposits to their owners, the IMF tried to protect the banks by demanding that the government intervene to block the legal process. Clearly the IMF only believes in the rule of law when it benefits its own interests. In practice its stance has been consistently against good governance and transparency, two of the theoretical pillars of its 'conditionality'. When it comes to changing laws, the IMF often weakens accountability – for example, requiring changes in the rules governing the Central Bank to provide legal immunity for its senior officials while enabling them to have more 'discretion' in paying IMF loans.

The IMF claims that its demands respond to absolute economic truth, but coincidentally the most acute pressure is always exerted during the run-up to a debt payment deadline. This pressure generates the urgency to sign an agreement, the contract in which the Fund primarily lends enough money to cover debts coming due. Its demands so blatantly rig the game for international interests that they make a mockery of the IMF's public discourse of improving the foundations of the national economy. One of the central demands in 2002 was that the government facilitate the transfer of dollars out of the country. Who might benefit from the measure? Foreign companies, wealthy individuals, and large national capital, keen to take their wealth in dollars abroad, increasing the chronic capital flight that Argentina has suffered for decades.

The Fund, an unaccountable, unelected institution, sees nothing wrong in forcing laws to be passed and repealed, infringing on national sovereignty and democracy. It demands macro-economic obedience, but nothing is too minor to escape its attention. An ongoing 'concern' IMF officials brought up on their visits was the leniency with which the government was dealing with people who after 2001 had not been able to keep up with their mortgage payments. The IMF demanded repossessions, which would effectively throw families out of their homes so that the banks could regain their assets. The government insisted that if the property belonged to a head of family and it was their sole home, it would not sanction a law to evict them. The IMF made noises that a long-term agreement could be in jeopardy over the government's stance.

In the aftermath of December 2001, the Fund was busy underlining that Argentina's problems were all self-created. Not only that, but when IMF officials put forward predictions of how the economy would behave in the following months, all the indicators were bleak: inflation would run riot, reserves would dwindle, and the currency would plummet. They refused to take the government's predictions seriously as a basis for an agreement, calling them over-optimistic.

Nobody would deny it was a bad year, but the IMF's predictions were seriously off the mark. In late 2002 Argentina's economic free fall began to plateau – after an entire year *without* an agreement with the IMF. There was growth for the first time in four years, exports were on the up, and post-devaluation inflation had been brought under control remarkably sooner than almost anyone had anticipated.

Given the number of crises in which the IMF has participated and its technical expertise, it might seem strange that it could be so wrong. But seen alongside the Fund's insistence on allowing foreign companies to buy up national bankruptcies, its miscalculation becomes clearer. The gatekeeper to international finance was announcing a bargain sale. Oscar Lamberto, the outgoing undersecretary for fiscal affairs in 2001 said in public what many thought: that the IMF's aim was for 'Argentina to explode and suffer a hyperinflation which will depreciate assets so that North American capital can come and buy our businesses for tuppence.'

Not that there was much left to buy, as foreign capital already owned over three quarters of national production (up from 46 per cent in 1963) and employed 56 per cent of the working population. Erosion in national ownership of industry had been accompanied by a marked deindustrialisation of the country. Fewer and fewer goods were produced internally because the strong currency of the 1990s made exports impossible and imports affordable. Because foreign ownership expanded while the range of industries contracted, the country became ever more dependent on foreign companies looking to make financial investments that would yield large margins and fast returns. So by 2003, there wasn't much left to sell. The crisis of 2001 meant the country's credit rating was atrocious, and the social situation remained precarious. What might the IMF propose?

More of the same, just in case the lesson had not been learnt. Yet something was different: on September 9th 2003 the existing agreement had expired and payment to the IMF itself came due. Everyone knows that you don't default on the IMF or the financial sky falls in. And yet Argentina did not pay. President Néstor Kirchner refused the conditions the IMF wanted to include in a new letter of intent. His message was, 'the country's economy has to grow for the debts to be paid,' and IMF austerity conditions endangered that growth. As *The Economist* put it, Horst Köhler, the head of the IMF, blinked first and went along with Argentina's self-assertion. Kirchner's stand was more symbolic than financial, especially since he agreed to a three per cent primary surplus (the budget surplus excluding interest payments on outstanding debt) that will be destined exclusively to debt payments. Still, the IMF didn't get the raise in tariffs it demanded (for its European senior shareholders), nor the 4.5 per cent surplus it wanted (which would have meant even greater cuts in spending), nor firm acquiescence that the government would compensate banks for devaluation.

It takes two to tango

As former broker Christian Stracke put it, when market analysts predicted Argentina's future, their motivation was to make a profit: 'they're in it for the money. If they were in it to be smart, they'd be professors.' He was talking to Paul Blustein of the *Washington Post*, who in 2003 exposed the role of Wall Street in pushing Argentina over the edge.[9]

It might seem obvious that 'market forces' are run on human decisions and the desire to make money. Still, the judgements made from financial centres and institutions are often taken as gospel truth, and the effects on poorer countries can be devastating. Usual practice is to state the good news and keep quiet the bad, all to encourage investors. Thus, Argentina was the shining example of how neo-liberal measures could tame inflation and bring stability. The shadow side of the dollar-peso peg was not mentioned: convertibility meant politicians could not print money, so to spend beyond their means they had only one option, to borrow.

And borrow they did. One would have expected the international markets to frown on the level of indebtedness and refuse Argentina more cash. But no, more debt meant more risk, which meant higher interest rates, which lead to bigger (short-term) profits. Even better for the international investors, Argentina borrowed by issuing bonds; for a time the government was the largest issuer of bonds of any emerging market. By 1998, the Asian crisis and its repercussions in Russia and Brazil meant that Argentina's bonds were a significant slice of the 'emerging market' business. Plus, the firms which arranged to float these bonds on the international market took fat commissions on top of the large gains made from high interest rates.

Kept out of the picture was the bad news: increasing unemployment and social unrest, and cheap imports and an overvalued peso that damaged national industry. Even exports were affected by a too-strong currency – they became too expensive to compete. Analysts who tried to sound a cautious note were forced to find themselves other, more rewarding jobs. As Blustein pointed out, 'investment bankers, analysts and bond traders served their own interests when they pumped up euphoria about the country's prospects.' He highlighted the example of 'a report published in October 2000 by J.P. Morgan, the biggest underwriter of Argentine bonds in the 1990s, titled, "Argentina's debt dynamics: Much ado about not so much."'

Another factor in the debacle in Argentina was the market mechanism with which Wall Street rates the performance of mutual fund and pension fund managers, both major buyers of Argentinian bonds. The rating system rewarded investment in those emerging markets with the biggest debts – and Argentina was often top of that list during the 1990s. Argentina's position meant that in the short term, bond traders had to invest in Argentina to make good returns that would ensure their bonuses. All this occurred in spite of acknowledgement by insiders that the industry index led to more lending to the most indebted, a perverse and irrational process.

From the point of view of Argentinian government officials, the markets' confidence reinforced their sense of being on the right track. After all, the most influential financial fraternity in the world couldn't be wrong, could it? It was easy to borrow and so they did. As with the 1970s debt crisis, Argentina's needs coincided with too much cash floating in the international system – liquidity looking to make profits. The misplaced optimism of financial bond giants like Goldman, Sachs & Co responds to more than a flaky system for evaluating managers: there are also large questions of conflict of interests. Blustein quoted Hans-Joerg Rudloff, chairman of the executive committee at Barclays Capital: 'the time has come to do our *mea culpa*; Argentina obviously stands as much as Enron [in proving that] things have been done and said by our industry which were realized at the time to be wrong, to be self-serving.'

The finance pundits were not punished for playing dangerous games with insider knowledge, and they are not even reprimanded for their most irresponsible behaviour. They gaily sold bonds to the 'consumer' market, to those individuals who buy and sell bonds on the stock exchange. If finance firms can be shown to have acted badly themselves, they stand guilty of deceiving small investors who do not have access to their knowledge. In 2003 there were considerable numbers of individual investors holding Argentinian bonds, including 400,000 in Italy and many thousands in Japan. The investors demanded a solution from the government, while those who had taken a commission for selling bonds they knew to be dodgy didn't get a mention.

As ever, the greedy market needed a local power broker to take up its game. As soon as Domingo Cavallo took over as economy minister for the second time in 2001, his good friend David Mulford, formerly of the US Treasury and then of the bank Credit Suisse, proposed a major bond deal, a 'mega-swap' to 'ease the debt'. The deal earned seven major banks, including Credit Suisse, HSBC and Citibank, US$150 million in commissions. And so the insane levels of debt were pushed up further. But debt bond traders were not the only perpetrators of the financial misdemeanours when they irresponsibly threw good money after bad.

Another crime appears to have been committed by the foreign banks operating in Argentina. In January 2002 the British paper *The Guardian* reported that two big UK banks had benefited handsomely from the crisis in Argentina. Suspicion was rife that banks played a significant and knowing part in capital flight.[10] Mario Cafiero, a left-of-centre deputy in the Argentinian Congress, accused HSBC and Lloyds of profiting from the crisis. They charged 'excessively high interest charges' and 'helped export US$130 billion of wealth through capital flight.' Cafiero reminded journalists that, 'fifty per cent of deposits were in the hands of foreign banks. British banks have to honour their debts to the people of Argentina, who entrusted them with US$6 billion of their savings and hard-earned money.' To add insult to injury, one in three bank employees has lost their job since the 2001 crisis.[11] Cases have been opened in Argentinian courts against a number of foreign banks. One judge, María Servini de Cubría, opened an investigation in 2003 against former President Fernando de la Rúa for an alleged crime of capital flight. During 2001, while he was in charge, the reserves of the Central Bank of Argentina decreased by an estimated US$18,000 million and bank deposits by 24 per cent.

The privatisation bonanza

Free marketeers complain that Latin America has been too timid in its embrace of neo-liberalism. They say that countries have privatised but not enough, and that they've kept too many important assets in the hands of the state. After all, Venezuela, Ecuador and Mexico still have their oil, and even Chilean dictator Augusto Pinochet didn't sell off Chile's copper.

Argentina, though, went the whole way, which is why it became the darling of the international markets even after it was clear that the economy was not sound. All the privatisations were done with little oversight, but some resulted in benefits for the consumer. Commercial services such as telecommunications were sold off and a better service ensued, although prices were higher. But the privatisation of natural resources and essential services was problematic in itself, as their social importance was greater – and the profit motive never improved services to the poor. Utilities like electricity and water were handed over, as were the airports and the ports. Banks were bought up, and the oil became foreign-owned. Even social security passed to private hands, at the insistence of the World Bank.

In 2003, President Kirchner announced that the government would review the contracts of all privatised services and companies, flagging up the woeful lack of regulation which had accompanied privatisation. Argentina privatised more than anyone else in Latin America and yet managed to make the least from it: according to the government, the total income during the 1990s from privatisations came to US$23,000 million. During the same time Brazil made US$71,000 million and Mexico US$31,750 million, even though they put much less up for sale.

It seems Argentina was sold cheap and, as it turns out, was robbed blind afterwards. First, international companies did not pay the entirety of the paltry prices negotiated but also 'bought debt'; these were financial transactions where the only winners were the brokers involved. Once installed as owners, companies did not invest as agreed. They raised tariffs so that they were higher than international rates, and during the ten years of convertibility, they effectively charged in dollars. They raised rates in relation to inflation in their home country if that was higher than in Argentina, as it mostly was. At least 70 per cent of their gains went straight out of the country and the economy.

The very near example of Chile did not serve to warn Argentinians of the dangers of losing all control over key sectors. Chile's wholesale adherence to neo-liberal economics under Pinochet's dictatorship had led to a spectacular crash in 1982 which increased poverty and inequality. Unemployment rose to over 22 per cent, poverty to 40 per cent, and the financial system, all in private hands, collapsed. Pinochet's response was to re-nationalise much of what had been sold off. And throughout it all, the main income-generating activity of the country, copper mining, remained in state hands. Copper mines had been nationalised in 1973 by the Allende government, and with them, Pinochet was able to pay his way from disastrous experiment to slow recovery.

In Argentina the bulk of privatisations were carried out between 1990 and 1994, a time too short to put in place the necessary regulation and checks on the transactions and contracts. The review of contracts announced by President Kirchner in 2003 had the rather modest aims of both finding out exactly how companies have failed to live up to their promises while accurately calculating their profits. the state's ignorance is revealing in itself

The lack of information reflects how Menem's government went about privatising. First the executive obtained extraordinary powers with a law of Economic Emergency, thus leaving Congress and other democratic institutions firmly out of the picture. Then Menem, his family, and the oligarchic interests he had surrounded himself with from the beginning of his mandate proceeded to carve out spoils much in the way medieval kings gave conquered lands to their barons.

The years of 'pizza and champagne', as they were known, were a festival of corruption fuelled by privatisation. The names of some of the buyers now ring bells of warning, but were grey anonymous corporate interests then, as was Enron, which bought the water system in Buenos Aires. Privatisation was undertaken with such zeal against the national interest that not only were the 'family heirlooms' sold for a song, but the nation even indebted itself in the process, as the state took on companies' debts so that the new private owners could make a profit from day one.

Daniel Aspiazu is an economist with the Facultad Latinoamericana de Ciencias Sociales (FLACSO) and he has researched in detail how privatisation was done and who benefited. He concludes that:

'In other countries, finite natural resources are not privatised [like in Argentina] and to make it worse, we hardly have any regulation. Companies are hardly investing in exploration, and the way they concentrate on exports, in ten years we'll be living by candlelight. We won't have oil or gas. We'll have to import it. Oil exports, which in 1991 were equivalent to about three per cent of production, at the moment surpass 40 per cent. It is madness. In most oil-exporting countries, companies cannot export unless they have guaranteed a certain amount of reserves. Here we don't even know if we have any reserves, because the four international consulting firms which audit reserves are financed by the private oil companies, so the state has no idea of how much oil and gas it really has. That is how far the dismantling of the state has gone.'[11]

As part of their package of loan conditions, the World Bank and IMF had been pressuring for privatisation since the 1980s, including the key area of oil, where Argentina was self-sufficient and a state monopoly operated through YPF (Yacimientos Petroleros Fiscales). President Alfonsín had already agreed in the 1980s to take a loan from the World Bank that required the state to prepare YPF for privatisation.

Selling off state enterprises to private capital put into motion dynamics which acquired a life of their own, exacerbated the country's depression, and worked against its economic recovery. These dynamics can be summed up as corruption, reduced state income, capital flight and more indebtedness. And that was only the financial impact. For society, private owners meant price hikes and more unemployment, all in return for (supposedly) improved efficiency – if the enterprise in question wasn't simply shut down, as happened to many railway lines. The logic of privatisation arose from Pinochet's claim of creating *'propietarios no proletarios'*, (owners not workers), and in a context in which jobs were fewer and fewer and inequality grew, the pro-capital and anti-social aim was evident.

Nothing was too valuable to sell off. In 1994, with natural resources handed over, Menem went on to privatise welfare, withdrawing the state from what some might argue is one of its main responsibilities. Aside from the social obligations shunned, the financial mechanisms entailed ruined the country. With social security contributions shifted into private hands, the government was deprived of a large amount of revenue it had used in the past to pay social costs due, pensions among them. As Dean Baker and Mark Weisbrot of the Center for Economic and Policy Research point out, according to IMF figures, 'the government lost an amount of revenue that has been estimated at 1.0 percent of annual GDP.'

The gap had to be filled, and new loans provided the only solution. Unfortunately, when the privatisation process began in 1994, a combination of a rise in interest rates in the US and the emerging market crises that began with Mexico in 1995 meant the interest on new credit was very high.[13]

Even if putting social security into private hands meant more efficient services (and that is in serious doubt), it also led to an unsustainable increase in debt to cover lost state income, which in turn contributed significantly to the eventual default in 2001. The fiscal deficit created by the loss of pension revenue meant that the IMF demanded a reduction in social spending to balance the books, and a 13 per cent cut was made in 2001. The result was a perverse circle of taking money from the poor to give to the rich, from the pensioners whom the state could no longer pay to the bankers abroad, while the bankers brokered the debt deals that gave the government cash to meet its pension obligations.

Why weren't Argentinian politicians worrying about what returns the country would see on the sale of state enterprises? Most were going along with Menem's popularity, but a number were speaking out about the levels of corruption surrounding privatisation. Politicians such as Elisa Carrió founded independent political careers on that basis (in her case, after belonging to the Radical party). But those near President Menem were too busy working out their own cut in the deals.

A case beloved of the media, involved one of Menem's closest collaborators, his minister for the environment and development, María Julia Alsogaray. In the first years of his government she was put in charge of privatising the state-run telecommunications company, known as ENTel. Why wait for the private owners to 'voluntarily' retire and sack workers when you can do it in advance for them? With 6,000 so dispatched, she ensured that ENTel installed 70 per cent fewer lines in 1990 than in 1989, and lines that were laid were not activated. On the back of these careful preparations, the new owners, Spanish Telefónica and French Telecom, were able to claim a commendable efficiency in their first year on the job. The fall in productivity had meanwhile reduced ENTel's price tag, while the new owners could charge higher rates indexed to the dollar.

In 2001, Alsogaray was under investigation for alleged illicit enrichment. Accusations were based on an increase in her patrimony from US$10,000 in 1990 to US$2,500 million in 2000. Suspicion surrounds possible overpayment to an ENTel creditor to the tune of US$10 million, while she has claimed in court that the overpayment was due to an accountant's error. Strangely, ENTel's accounting records dating from 1988 have been lost. The list of irregularities is long and Alsogaray has twenty court cases open against her. And she is only the better known of a roster of politicians and officials who managed privatisations. In 2000, over a hundred people were being processed for similar charges by the Anti-Corruption Office of the Ministry of Justice.[14]

Roots of discontent

The year 1989 was a defining one for the country: hyper-inflation brought neurosis, the spectres of unemployment and hunger dominated the social landscape and President Menem proposed tough measures as the only way forward. It was also the year he issued the first presidential pardon for those not covered by the laws of Punto Final and Obediencia Debida. The Madres de Plaza de Mayo were more and more often called 'las locas', the madwomen. Democracy had not proved to be a panacea.

Yet something else was going on, too. Many new social groups sprang up in the aftermath of 1989. Their work didn't bear public fruit during the first heady years of stability, when the economy grew at unheard of rates. But already by 1992, discontent with the structures of power began to crystallise. That was the year the forerunner to the Central de los Trabajadores Argentinos (CTA), began to organise specifically to counter Menem's neo-liberal policies. It was a moderate independent union movement formed by leaders of teachers' and state workers' unions who broke with the Confederación General de Trabajadores (CGT), a bastion of Peronism and corruption. The CTA was organised along more democratic lines internally, with local and secret votes; by 2003 it could count on 860,000 individual affiliated members.

The Madres, with their enduring conviction, never stopped, in spite of political and strategic differences which meant a division of the movement into three in the 1980s: the Asociación de Madres led by Hebe Bonafini, the Madres Línea Fundadora (Founding Line), led by a group of mothers, and the Abuelas de Plaza de Mayo, a group of mothers who decided to concentrate on the task of recovering the children stolen from their sons and daughters. In the mid 1990s the children of some of those disappeared began to organise, too, and support human rights work with a generational renewal. Demands to end impunity were heard among the young and were slowly re-integrated by society. They were helped by the publication in 1995 of the first confession of someone involved in the military repression, Alfredo Scilingo, who poured out his guilty conscience to journalist Horacio Verbitsky.

The Madres were at the front line of protest, from the time nobody dared show their discontent (they began their silent marches in 1977) through the brief years in the early 1980s when democracy appeared capable of bringing justice, and throughout the wilderness years of amnesty for the perpetrators of state terror. For over a quarter of a century they have been the conscience of Argentina. Since the laws of Punto Final and Obediencia Debida were passed, political discourse had been about 'forgetting and moving on'. But human rights groups, which number many more than the Madres, together have formed a constant resistance against forgetting, reminding society that it is impossible to live and thrive in a state which illegally murdered 30,000 citizens.

By 1995 their endurance began to come back into fashion and their oppositional stance was shared with many emerging groups. It was the year of uprisings in various provinces to protest non-payment of state employees and generalised political corruption. The traditional and new union movements came together to call for a general strike, while the new progressive party FREPASO (Frente País Solidario, Country in Solidarity Front) and the Radicals organized a five-minute cacerolazo and blackout against government measures, a citizens' protest whose repercussions they could not foresee.

In 1997 teachers in the cities of Neuquén and Buenos Aires called for a march and a fast to protest a new education law. The popular support which greeted them took them by surprise, although official indifference didn't. To minimise the impact of their protest on their supporters they decided not to leave the classrooms but to create a permanent fast in front of Congress, where a few teachers at a time would protest. To shelter from the oncoming winter they rented a white marquee which eventually became their trademark, the *'carpa blanca'*. The success of the protest seemed to fire off other 'new' forms of protest, more imaginative and more inclusive than past confrontations – the key to the success of the carpa blanca was bringing protesters and supporters together in a space where solidarity could be expressed.

The solidarity and the upsurge in mobilisation made visible the *Tercer Sector* (third sector, not government, not business): civil society, community organisations and NGOs – and it grew steadily throughout the 1990s. Many organisations had been created after 1989, when social problems became increasingly acute. By 2003, according to the Justice Ministry, there were 78,000 duly registered groups, although it is estimated many more work informally. A national poll ascertained that 3.5 million people (almost ten per cent of the population) carried out some form of voluntary work, while more than half of households had donated money during 2002.

The move away from trusting that the state and traditional forms of power could solve social problems did not begin in 2001. The same Gallup poll found that 60 per cent of those asked trusted not-for-profit community organisations over politicians or trade unions; by 2001, the third sector was already employing more than 300,000 people. As neo-liberal policies encouraged the state to shun its responsibilities, social endeavours grew. Many carry out basic welfare provision, or pick up where the state has left off or has never been at all. For this reason many organisations are considered apolitical, and most indeed are. Yet many go beyond charity and reclaim a public role for individuals who have been socially, as well as politically, disenfranchised by unemployment and individualism.[15]

Politics was not immune to all the fervent in society. The explosion of 2001 might lead to that assumption but during the 1990s political processes did reflect the social problems the population was struggling with – but were signally unable to improve matters.

One might be forgiven for thinking that in Argentina politics is a two-party game: together with the military, the Peronists and Radicals have dominated twentieth-century politics. Yet there are upward of two dozen political parties, many of them small groups but recognised players in national politics.

The most important development in the 1990s was a coming together of left and social democratic leaders, both from within the established parties and from the smaller left and nationalist parties. In 1993 the Frente Grande (Large Front) was formed, a forerunner to the creation in December 1994 of the FREPASO. This latter front for solidarity had been created by dissident Peronists and Radicals, the Unidad Socialista, and various small left and populist parties. They were the first to express politically the inchoate dissatisfaction with the neo-liberal revolution. Without disowning the economic policies, they put the emphasis on social problems, a renewal in politics and ethical questions such as corruption and the weakness of institutions. The FREPASO showed great political promise when it came in second to Menem in the presidential elections of 1995, displacing the Radicals from their usual place. Yet it never managed to consolidate a national party structure and it was, as historian Luis Alberto Romero calls it, 'a party of leaders'. José Bordón, the presidential candidate, came from provincial Peronism; he left after the 1995 vote. His place was taken by Carlos 'Chacho' Alvarez, supported by Graciela Fernández Meijide, who had a background in human rights work, and Aníbal Ibarra, who would eventually go on to become the mayor of Buenos Aires in 2000 and 2003.

After their electoral success, instead of consolidating their 'political renewal' appeal, members of the FREPASO began to work closely with the Radicals in parliament and began discussions towards broader collaboration. In 1997 they launched the Alianza para la Justicia, el Trabajo y la Educación

– the Alliance for Justice, Work and Education. The FREPASO's appeal, mostly to the centre-left of the electorate, joined an old and efficient party machine; the UCR acquired instant 'renovation' which helped Radical Fernando de la Rúa to win the 1999 presidential election, with Chacho Alvarez as his vice president. Together the UCR and FREPASO gained the middle ground, but the country lost an alternative to the two main parties, and the sense of loss only grew as disenchantment with formal politics built up to 'que se vayan todos'.

Notes

1   Calcagno A.E. and E. Calcagno. 'El precio de la convertibilidad, encrucijada de la economía argentina,' *Le Dipló*, Buenos Aires Nº 8, February 2000

2   Interview by Duncan Green, CAFOD (the official Catholic aid agency for England and Wales)

3   Stiglitz, J. 'Argentina Shortchanged', *Washington Post*, May 12 2002, http://www.washingtonpost.com/ac2/wp-dyn?pagename=article& node=&contentId=A3893-2002May10&notFound=true

4   *Clarín*, January 13 2002

5   http://www.imf.org/external/about.htm

6   Palast, Greg, 'Today's winner of the Nobel Prize in economics,' *The Observer*, October 10 2001

7   http://www.imf.org/

8   http://alainet.org/active/show_news.phtml?news_id=4406

9   Blustein P. 'Argentina didn't fall on its own', *Washington Post*, August 3 2003. http://www.washingtonpost.com/wp-dyn/articles/A15438-2003 Aug2_4.html

10 Elliott L. and J. Treanor 'British banks profited from Argentina's woes' *The Guardian*, January 15 2002

11 *Página/12*, August 11 2003

12 Aspiazu, D. (Ed.) 2002, *Privatizaciones y poder económico, la consolidación de una sociedad excluyente*, Quilmes, Universidad Nacional de Quilmes

13 Baker D. and Weisbrot M. 'The role of social security privatization in Argentina's economic crisis', 2002, see http://www.cepr.net/ argentina_and_ss_privatization.htm

14 http://www.quepasa.cl/revista/2000/08/20/t-21.08.QP.MUN. MARIJULIA.html

15 *Desafíos Urbanos*, Año 7 No. 33, May/June 2001

4
High Hopes

'We are contributing to the birth of a new sociability, a new subjectivity, however you want to call it.'
Pablo Solana, MTD Lanús[1]

Self-appointed agents of change

At first glance, a curious tourist might see a street party in the gathering of young people with whistles and drums. A closer look at their serious faces and a second look at the placards might reveal the protest they embody. The participants' fierce chants are part denunciation, but also reflect their hurt and anger and, curiously, celebrate their being there at all.

This is an *escrache*, a new form of protest pioneered by the sons and daughters of the disappeared. In the face of the impunity enjoyed by those guilty of state terrorism during the last dictatorship, they have tried to bring their own blast of justice to the perpetrators. An escrache is the public outing and shaming of those known to have participated in the death and torture of thousands of their compatriots.

Victims of state terrorism in Argentina can still bump into their torturers on the street. In 1995 the son of a disappeared man happened upon former naval captain Alfredo Astiz, known as 'the Angel of Death', and could not but tell the friends he went on to meet. Together they carried out the first spontaneous public repudiation of a repressor. Soon more such events were organised and in the following months a new network of activists came together: HIJOS, Hijos por la Identidad y la Justicia Contra el Olvido y el Silencio (Sons and daughters for identity and justice and against silence and forgetting). A new generation had become part of the human rights movement. It was the beginning of a public re-engagement with the years of dictatorship, which the majority of society had buried as events to be forgotten and left behind.

Escraches and other forms of protest in the mid-1990s had one defining shared characteristic: 'doing it for yourself.' When institutions will not and can not deliver justice, find the repressor and shame him publicly. When companies go bust in the economic crises, take over the sources of employment and keep producing. When the state will not regulate the economy so that people can find work, organise your own productive projects, as did many MTDs, *movimientos de trabajadores desempleados,* (unemployed workers' movements). When the government has ceased to listen to the people, turn out in the thousands to create pot and pan pandemonium.

A new word has been created to express the DIY nature of much social organising: *autoconvocados,* meaning self-organised, often, though not exclusively, among those who did not already belong to an established group. A new breed of political activist has appeared, one who takes pride in not belonging to a political party, trade union, or other group. This attitude blames associations, such as trade unions, for collaborating with the political system being repudiated; it also justifies voting for right-wing candidates who are not formally politicians. The most hopeful manifestation of this trend is that many of the most active and energetic people working for social change were previously only spectators of social and political processes.

The salient originality of the protest which took to the streets on December 19th and 20th 2001 was that no one had called for it to happen – not the trade unions, the NGOs, nor the Madres de Plaza de Mayo, not the political parties, nor the media. The anger and frustration which bubbled over on that hot night arose from each citizen's personal experience, only to find a loud echo of recognition in millions of others. As the din of pot-banging attracted ever more participants, each was aware of shared disgust and fury at the situation in which they found the country and themselves. It was an immediate and direct experience of being part of society, a temporary short-circuit which connected people usually separated by class, by the media they consume, and by sheer indifference to the plight of others. In spite of being mainly a Buenos Aires affair, the importance of the Argentinazo has been felt across the country – its weight likened to that of the Cordobazo in defining the end of an era.

At the time, the mood was a strange mix of anger and celebration. Celebratory was the sense of having found a voice, a way that allowed ordinary people to be heard. The big cacelorazo had been a call to action. The Argentinazo was an exultant reminder of the people to themselves that power can reside with the ordinary folk, rather than the anointed few. The crowd of thousands who turned out in the heat of mid-summer December was so diverse as to defy general description and explanation. Likewise, the increasing level of involvement of people in local and national matters is well exemplified by, but not only reduced to, the new types of organisation which have received some coverage in the media: barter clubs, the organised unemployed known as *piqueteros*, neighbourhood assemblies, and worker-occupied factories.

These may appear to be dispersed and unrelated forms of dissent. However, a look at the methods employed by groups as dissimilar as the piqueteros, the neighbourhood assemblies and the workers who have taken over factories shows some common threads: a sense of the failure of representative politics, attempts at a wide range of experiments in direct democracy, and, more broadly, a shared understanding of having to roll up one's sleeves and muck in for anything to truly change.

The loud chant of the cacerolazos, 'que se vayan todos,' out with the lot of them, was directed at the entire political class and all those entrusted to run the nation. It had become clear that politicians could not be trusted and that the population at large bore an element of responsibility for not resisting or shaping their policies sufficiently. Ironically, the political parties in opposition to Menem had organised the first cacerolazos in 1995. Society took up these noisy protests enthusiastically and by 2001 felt them to be firmly 'outside the system', enough so to use them to oust Fernando de la Rúa's Alianza government.

In the first days of January 2002, the neighbourhood assemblies were born when groups of neighbours continued to take to the streets but began to put down their saucepans, to organise themselves and to ask, 'what kind of country do we want?' The rejection of representation as a gut reaction provided a new starting point, because from that feeling flowed an understanding of the need for each citizen to take responsibility in some way. The attempts to have debates on the street and open to all demanded some structure, yet people agreed to have no leaders, no representatives, no structure. They called it 'horizontality', the opposite of hierarchy, rank and leadership. And so the debates that raged fiercely covered everything from the causes of the national problems to the nature of politics and how to be a member of the polity and of the assembly itself. The challenge of making the assemblies work – which met with mixed success – sharpened participants' understanding of the complexity and potential of political life.

As important as the novel forms of protest was the sense that these were accompanied by a shift in attitudes. There was a move away from the individualism of silence and eyes averted from others' misfortune that reigned during the terror of the dictatorship and the rule of neo-liberalism, to an understanding that 'we're all in it together'. The upsurge in social solidarity was expressed even across social classes and was made explicit in the slogan '*piquete y cacerolas, la lucha es una sola*' (roadblocks and saucepans, the struggle is one and the same). The new links between the more working-class piqueteros and the mostly middle-class neighbourhood assemblies was a sign of the growing recognition that there can be no cohesive society when so many are excluded.

For the majority of the population, new social relations manifested themselves in non-political forms of solidarity, the everyday refusal to ignore others' misfortune. Even *La Nación*, the main conservative daily, introduced a new listing in its classified section: the Solidarity Network, where not-for-profit institutions can offer and seek support – free ads in one of the country's premier national listings. And even if most of the activities listed are traditionally 'charitable' (known as 'assisten-tialism' in Argentina) and often derided by more politicised activists, they are a welcome change from a national culture which explicitly approved of looking out for number one.

The number of people willing to participate in new social initiatives has been great, and was building up before the crisis exploded. In mid-December 2001, millions of citizens voted in a popular referendum organised by the Frente Nacional Contra la Pobreza, FRENAPO (National Front Against Poverty) on the creation of a monthly unemployment benefit of 380 pesos (then equal to dollars), child benefit and a basic pension. The CTA helped found FRENAPO and presented the project to Congress. When the legislature failed to take it up, the CTA helped provide the infrastructure to conduct the vote anyway. At more than three million, the number of votes was higher than that garnered by the Alianza just two months earlier in the October 2001 parliamentary elections. In contrast, few wanted to vote in the official election, and because voting is obligatory, 60 per cent of the ballots cast were blank or 'angry', that is, damaged voting papers. The massive turnout for the FRENAPO vote underscored that it is not democracy people object to, but the lack of real choice at the ballot box. The consultation fired the imagination of millions who made an effort to cast their vote in spite of minimal 'electoral' infrastructure and funding.

FRENAPO brought together a novel range of organisations, from universities to small business groups, independent trade unions, human rights groups and cultural NGOs. Individual intellectuals, artists and activists joined the campaign, as did a few politicians from the left and those distinguished by their struggles against political corruption, such as Elisa Carrió of the ARI party, Argentinos por una República de Iguales (Argentinians for a Republic of Equals). Organising for the FRENAPO vote facilitated the coming together of new local groups and created networks across organisations that would be called upon during the mass mobilisations of 2002.

Together they discovered that pressure pays, although not well. A few months after the consultation,[2] the government responded by introducing the *Plan Jefas y Jefes de Hogar* (heads of households family benefit) of 150 Lecops, (a parallel currency, equal to the peso, emitted by the national government). By 2002 this subsidy was worth only US$60. And although some three million people applied for the benefit in a matter of weeks, it took two years for only half of the requests to be processed.

The social effervescence that had been building up during the 1990s was strengthened and moved forward by the Argentinazo. Yet at the same time, the uprising's tumultuous aftermath suffered from the lack of capacity of civil society to absorb or channel the massive need for citizen participation and collective solidarity it evoked. By the end of 2002, it was apparent that the level of engagement was dropping, if one looked at the numbers involved in public actions. How much of what happened in the run-up and in those powerful days in December had a longer, deeper impact? What remained after all that mobilisation? What had changed?

What follows is an overview of the most innovative forms of social action which appeared with or were reinforced by the crisis.

'Piqueteros'

When forced out of work, people lose their purpose, their livelihood, their social networks and their self-esteem. The popular image of the unemployed person is that he or she sits at home, depressed, ground down by the exclusion from economic life, a plight affecting all urban societies from the most to the least developed.

In Argentina, though, some unemployed workers have been creating a different image for themselves. They are enacting the most powerful and original form of organisation practiced since the triumph of neo-liberalism in the 1990s: piquetes, or road-blocks. They cannot picket their factory, because they lost their jobs long ago. Jorge Valles, member of a group in San Francisco Solano in the province of Buenos Aires, explains: 'the factories no longer exist, they are all closed. The workers are in the neighbourhoods. For this reason we say that the neighbour-hood is the big factory and the road is the factory gate.'[3] They are known as 'piqueteros', and a radical minority refer to themselves as MTDs (unemployed workers' movements).

Those displaced by society and the economy have placed themselves at the heart of everyday activity: on streets, bridges and highways. Roads are the arteries of commerce, and mobility a right everyone takes for granted. Piqueteros block roads because it is the only way anyone will listen to their problems, their last resort. They don't close roads for the sake of disruption, although angry motorists and anyone who depends on moving goods or people might disagree. Back in the shantytowns where many piqueteros live, nobody paid any notice to them whatsoever. Their actions are the only way they have found to become visible to society. Instead of passively accepting their fate, they are active; they force others into immobility to make themselves noticed.

There are over a dozen nationally-organised piquetero movements and MTDs, although many more local groups operate both independently and in coalition with others. Many participants are very young, though all generations mingle on the tarmac. The public image portrayed by the media is of a young man, face covered with a scarf or t-shirt, next to burning tyres, although across the organisations of the unemployed eight out of ten active members are women and piquetes are non-violent protests. They build blockades to force those in power to listen to them, and then they go home to continue discussing, working together and organising for change in their locality and beyond.

It is hard to keep up with their activities. Estimates of the number of roadblocks differ wildly and the media only really 'see' those near towns or where violence erupts as police repression is turned on. A rough estimation is that there were some 140 roadblocks in 1997. With each passing year the number grew, and in 2002 there were anything between 2,300 and 6,000, depending on the source.

Broadly, three types of organisations have arisen: politically-independent MTDs that have their beginnings in myriad grassroots organisations such as squatter groups and Christian base communities; groups created or run by radical left parties; and those organised via independent unions, such as the ones associated with the CTA and the Corriente Clasista y Combativa, CCC (Combative and Classist Current).

The latter groups, which also include a variety of squatter organisations and groups such as the Federación de Tierra, Vivienda y Habitat, FTV (Land, Housing and Habitat Federation), comprise the largest and best-resourced block of piqueteros. The CTA is the first national trade union movement to include the unemployed, which has allowed it to carve out new political space. The CTA and CCC are also the most integrated into the existing political system, with political links including socialist and nationalist parties. A newspaper put their share of the piquetero movement at around two thirds of the total.[4] Those aligned with far-left parties probably mobilise over 20 per cent of piqueteros, while the most politically independent and anti-systemic groups make up the rest.

Although they all use road blockades as a bargaining tool, there are substantial differences in the methods and aims of each current. The majority, under the banner of the CTA, are workers with no work who use the federation to reclaim their lost jobs and claw back some rights. They look back to a time in living memory when there were enough jobs to go round, and demand that the state restore their place in society as workers with social rights. They also bring together progressive sectors of society who support their initiatives.

Their vision may seem idealistic in an age of receding employment generation. Yet many believe they stand a better chance of achieving their objectives than that part of the movement with links or roots in the far left. The latter groups believe road-blocks are the beginning of a revolutionary process of taking over the state, and for that reason are the most critical of existing politicians.

Meanwhile, the smallest current of autonomous MTDs is known as the toughest, not normally as a compliment. Their reputation is born of their marginal status, the middle-class fear of the shantytowns, and their long-term poverty and reported violence. They also refer to themselves as tough, in the sense of both uncompromising and able to defend themselves from the police repression with which they are all too familiar. Autonomy is their main aim, and even though most depend on welfare programmes to support their organisations, they stress the need to become independent of that help.

The MTDs are not taken very seriously by the established powers, including the media, due partly to the marginality of those they represent and partly to their non-engagement in party politics. Yet their logic, based on the belief that the state will never again provide for all and that capitalism as they know it does not need them, may be an accurate reading of reality. And so they reject putting effort into integrating with national politics and instead concentrate on building themselves up through training, collective work and networking. They aim for the transformation of members' lives, bringing together politics and the everyday. They hold that such is the route to a profound change in understanding, which will lead to real social change in the future.

All the piquetero movements share more characteristics than they would perhaps admit themselves. Many do not relish having to resort to roadblocks to survive. Organising pickets gives them a purpose and a community, but they do not want to be known only as 'piqueteros'. They want to be known as women and men seeking work and dignity, not a handout. María Itatí Gómez of a CTA-affiliated group in the province of Buenos Aires expresses how many feel: 'yes, it helps us emotionally, you have a space where you can express your anger; but in another sense it is not a source of dignity. We do not like going to block the road. We do not feel this gives us power. We do it out of necessity. People do not say, "Ay, I feel dignified because I blocked a road." We do it because it is necessary because we are not heard. What we need is a job, one that is dignified.'[5] Their varied approaches reflect the range of analyses and responses piquetero groups make to their situations, and more broadly, the division in strategies across all social movements. The main element they have in common is the method of blocking roads.

The founding experience of using roadblocks took place in 1996 when residents of the towns of Cutral Có and Plaza Huincul in the southern province of Neuquén rose up against the local authorities. These towns had been built around the work provided by YPF, the state oil company. When it was privatised in 1991 those families lost their lifeline. Four thousand workers were laid off in one go and more jobs disappeared slowly. Thousands had their gas and electricity cut off. There was little in the way of redundancy payments or benefits and nothing in the way of new jobs. When negotiations to open a fertilizer factory, that would have provided 50 jobs, fell through, a mass protest swept through the area, fanned by calls emitted by the local radio, which was owned by a member of the opposition to the provincial government.

It was mid-winter and the temperature hovered around zero as thousands of women, men and children built five major pickets and many more smaller obstacles, cutting off access to the towns. They remained on the barricades for seven days and six nights. On the morning of June 25th, a judge and 400 soldiers of the national *gendarmería* arrived to clear the roads – this militarised police force is feared as it has historically been used to repress popular protest. Brute force got the gendarmería through the first picket, but as they approached the second, 20,000 locals marched toward them from the opposite direction – around half of the total population. The judge heading the clearance ordered the armed forces to halt.

The next day, a group of picket representatives and Laura Padilla, their spokesperson, met with the provincial governor, Felipe Sapag. The meeting had been their main demand during the long days out in the cold. Sapag signed a document agreeing to all their points, including a 'state of social emergency', jobs in state works, food parcels for those in need, and no reprisals against those involved in the protests, among other things. Their example was quickly taken up. The next year a roadblock was constructed in Buenos Aires and the protestors achieved their aim of receiving state aid in the form of income maintenance in exchange for community service.[6]

In 2002, the main benefit available to those with no work and no income was the Plan Jefas y Jefes de Hogar (Heads of Household Benefit) subsidy of 150 pesos a month while the basic food needs of a family have been calculated to cost 329 pesos. Two thirds of those collecting the benefit are women. The subsidy comes with strings attached: in return for an amount that does not cover a family's food requirements, recipients are expected to do 20 hours of 'community work'. In many cases local councils and the political party in power use this enforced labour to carry out public works. The subsidy is also used to 'encourage' political allegiance, or discourage participation in more radical groups.

The organisations of the unemployed have different attitudes and practices in relation to the work plans. Many piquetero organizations receive a certain number of subsidies that they then administer. In general the work hours demanded are carried out within the piquetero organisation, contributing to its development or projects. The subsidies are a recruitment incentive, a way in which people become involved. For families on the edge of survival, the organisation is seen as a route to obtaining a 'Plan' and they do not mecessarily join into the communal activities beyond their enforced 20 hours. Similarly, although the plans fit into a wider web of political clientelism, it is adapted to specific local circumstances. Some groups do demand political participation from those obtaining the Plan through them, although many leave that up to the conscience of each person.

The piqueteros are accused in the press (and by extension, by the public at large) of 'buying' people with the Plans, and in turn, having been co-opted themselves by the politicians who give them control over a certain number of Plans. Local politicians do buy support with the benefits, but in general political parties tend to compete with the piquetero groups rather than operate through them. Mistrust runs deep in all directions and alliances are much rarer than cleavages and confrontation. In practice the Plans are an aid to organisation, but not the cause of it. Being on the receiving end of less than two dollars per day does not make everyone feel beholden to the giver – particularly not in view of the significant resources the state invests in police-led repression against their protests.

That repression begins with labelling, with some piqueteros portrayed as soft, others as hard-line. Not coincidentally, the latter adjective is attached to those most critical and distant from party politics. Then the threats begin, and the intimidation, and the arrests under trumped-up charges. The CTA states that thousands of unemployed workers throughout Argentina, many of whom are jailed, are facing charges for having participated in roadblocks. These arrests contribute to a wider strategy of criminalisation of social protest.

Murder has also been used as a form of collective intimidation. Protestors have been killed at the hands of the police, without any justifiable provocation – in each case the victims were unarmed and many shot in the back. The fallen are remembered in the names of new piquetero groups which have adopted them: Teresa Rodríguez was the first known victim, killed in Neuquén in 1997, while Aníbal Verón was blocking a road in Salta when he was shot. Both are now household names due to the groups that bear their names.

On June 26th 2002, a roadblock took place on the Pueyrredón bridge, an important access to Buenos Aires from the southern district of Avellaneda. The well-organised and disciplined road blockers were no strangers to harassment and threats by the police, in uniform and out of it. That day, two young men were shot dead at close range. After the incident President Eduardo Duhalde blamed strife among piqueteros. However, within 24 hours of the shootings photographic evidence and testimonies showed that police officers had carried out the brutal murders of Darío Santillán and Maximiliano Kosteki.

The MTD of Lanús, to which Darío had belonged, published a book in 2002 entitled *Darío y Maxi, Dignidad Piquetera* (Darío and Maxi, Piquetero Dignity). In it they investigate the events leading up to their deaths. They underline the planned and coordinated repression they all suffered that day; victims also included 33 wounded with lead bullets. Yet the police officers identified as responsible for the violence were free, on the run from justice, although by the middle of 2003 some of the officers identified had been detained or were in the midst of court proceedings.

Darío Santillán,
interviewed by Hernán López Echagüe

'We are not proposing to represent anyone. We're clear about that. We only offer the possibility to struggle to get 'Planes Trabajar' [social security] ... Ours is a movement under construction. We don't know how things will turn out. We are against the concept of power. Inside our organisation there are no leaders. We are all the same and we vote in assemblies about what to do next. We think the most important things are education and consciousness, and that's why we run training workshops. Until the people, who have 500 years of domination upon them, begin to understand that everything can be different, there will be no possibility of real change.'[8]

The massive police operation that left Santillán and Kosteki dead shocked and outraged the country, and their deaths were taken by many as an attack on the whole of the progressive social movements. MTD Lanús was part of a coordination called 'Aníbal Verón' that includes other local MTDs; among them they mobilise some 5,000 people.[7] The day after the murders, tens of thousands marched with the piqueteros to show their solidarity and support. The 26th of June has become a day of remembrance and struggle, a time to focus the public eye on the ongoing repression protestors face daily.

What is it about the piqueteros that draws such fire from the current structure of power? On the one hand, they are simply vulnerable groups, cast out sectors of society that have always been at the receiving end of police brutality and a trigger-happy attitude toward security. On the other hand, they raise deeper questions of social control and the fact that the poverty at the root of the piquetero protest now engulfs over half of the population. Those in power know there are good grounds for their protest to become generalised, which would be uncontainable. Hence all means, legal or illegal, are used to combat them even while they only represent a fraction of those affected by increasing poverty. All this in a context where the repressive apparatus of the state has not been reformed or purged since the last dictatorship.

Unlike during the 1970s, the police are not responding to any form of direct attack on themselves or institutionality. There have been discussions as to the legality of road blocks, which perhaps surprisingly, have not been pursued by politicians. This struggle is ideological, and at its heart are the MTD demands to be allowed to organise, that the poor be given the opportunity to become fully in charge of their lives, collectively and on their own terms. As such, the MTDs challenge traditional sources of authority and highlight how state neglect has bred a tough mistrust of established power. As Julio Ferreyra, a member of MTD Lanús, puts it: 'our principles are horizontality, autonomy and direct democracy, with that we want to create power to achieve social change. Our aim is to build from the grassroots. I'm not a leader, I'm here on the assembly's mandate. We draw on "leading by obedience" as Subcomandante Marcos says.'[1]

The piqueteros in and around the capital get the most attention, but this was a rural movement to begin with and blocking rural roads continues to grow as a tool of protest. One organisation that added roadblocks to its repertoire of struggle was the MOCASE, the Movimiento Campesino de Santiago del Estero (Smallholder Movement of Santiago del Estero, a town in the north of the country). These families have endured 12 years of intimidation and paramilitary violence at the hands of the provincial authorities and the corrupt landowners who try to throw them off their land illegally. The methods of choice are to burn crops and houses, to kill cattle and put up fencing in the night – all against mostly subsistence farmers who have worked the land for nearly a century. The 9,600 families who are part of MOCASE have survived the onslaught only because they work collectively.

In his book '*La política está en otra parte*' (Politics is else-where), journalist Hernán López Echagüe recounts meetings with members and leaders of MOCASE. This is the story of Paulo Aranda, of Pozo del Toba.

'Now we know that we have the law on our side, and because we've worked the land for over twenty years, since 1925, the land is ours. But the businessmen, the judiciary, the powerful, they don't care about the law. They frame you. They try to pay you off individually. The first thing they do is offer you money, they want to buy your right to the property. My brother has been threatened to death, with a gun. They threatened me, saying they would burn down my house with me and my family in it. In fact they did, when I was away working and my wife visiting family, they burnt down our house where the cotton harvest was stored, four thousand kilos of cotton we had to sell, all burnt. It was in August 1995. I think it was the local businessmen. Sometimes you can hardly believe it. The owners make the threats and the police just let them get on with it. I don't know what it is, if there's money flowing between them, but the fact is that they're free and we've reported it all, they killed our animals, and the bullets found in them sit in some police drawer gathering dust.'[10]

MOCASE, the MTDs, the CTA and CCC – these are some of the piqueteros in crude brushstrokes. Looked at in detail, every group is unique. To prove that a short summary such as this cannot successfully convey the diversity among local piquetero groups, one example may help. Researcher Dennis Rodgers spent time with the MTD in La Matanza in the province of Buenos Aires, which distinguished itself from other groups by deciding not to accept the government subsidies that sustain others' work. Their stand led their numbers to diminish greatly, but the numerical decline has been accompanied by an increased interest and respect for their activities. Their reasoning was straightforward: they don't want to be sucked into the clientelistic Peronist politics that surround the govern-ment handouts. They do accept funding from abroad, and are using it to launch a variety of projects such as a cooperative bakery and other social enterprises. As with other new social movements, academics and sympathizers form a constant stream of visitors. What the members of this MTD do with the interest is instructive of their level of internal debate: they have set up swaps with academic departments seeking to carry out research 'on' them, and they get classes on social work and sociology in return for being case studies.[11]

Recovered factories, workers' control

> *'If I only stay at home I'm going to die. There, in my house, I'm the living dead, nobody is going to give me a job at my age, I'm 48, I'm old, but I have a lot of experience.'*
> Eduardo, a mechanic fighting to re-open a factory to produce spaghetti [Sasetru][12]

In the context of an economic depression, bankruptcies of businesses went from a trickle in the mid 1990s to a flood by 2001. Tens thousands of workers have managed to turn around the scourge of unemployment by taking over the means of production for themselves. There had been isolated instances of workers taking over sources of work since at least the 1980s. But in the late 1990s many more workers began to do it for themselves: taking over their workplace when factories went bankrupt or the owners decided to close down. They call it 'recovering' the factories, keeping them alive to provide jobs. An estimated 120 factories have been reclaimed by their workers, safeguarding some 12,000 jobs.

One of the pioneers in taking over and putting a factory under workers' control was Industrias Metalúrgicas y Plásticas Argentina, IMPA (Metals and Plastics Industry of Argentina) in the centre of Buenos Aires. It was closed by the management in 1997 but now employs 174 people. The workers restarted the only aluminium manufacturing plant in the country and at the same time created a cultural centre, the Factory Cultural City, which has become a point of reference for many of the new social organisations. The cultural space became a focus of interaction with society and at times a crucial survival mechanism, a place from where solidarity links were forged at difficult times in the process of establishing worker management.

At IMPA all workers earn the same amount, some 900 pesos per month (US$310 at the 2003 exchange rate) and decisions are taken collectively in assemblies. There is an ongoing discussion about pay differentials but these have not been worked out yet. The company was established by German immigrants at the beginning of the twentieth century, and it was then nationalised in the 1940s. It became a co-operative in 1961, although this status was a legal fig leaf behind which the company accentuated disparities between management and shop floor workers. Over 1997 and 1998 there was an attempt by the management to strip the company of its assets, but the workers resisted the move.

IMPA is unusual among recovered factories in that it was already a co-operative in legal terms, so the workers could easily take over management of the company. For 36 years the legal structure that should have enabled worker participation had been successfully used to keep them out of decisions and underline their lowly status. IMPA has become an inspiration for workers occupying and recovering factories across the country, even though not all recovered factories have chosen to become cooperatives.

IMPA is now a member of a national network of occupied factories created in early 2002, the Movimiento Nacional de Empresas Recuperadas, MNER (National Movement of Recovered Companies), which brought together around 70 enterprises travelling the long road from owner bankruptcy to worker-led functioning. One of MNER's tasks has been to improve the legal framework for factory takeovers. The existing Bankruptcy Law gives precedence to the creditors over the employees, something MNER has sought to reverse. An amendment they have lobbied for would allow for the company's assets to be given to the workers for two years rather than be auctioned to pay debts.

The pioneering role of IMPA workers has proved invaluable for those who came later. They have provided advice, lawyers and experience to many factories taken over since 2001. Their model of enmeshing themselves in the social fabric around them has also been noted and encouraged elsewhere. Support from society at large has been the defining factor in the survival of many enterprises.

According to Cándido González, one of the members of the Chilavert printing co-operative, 'it's not like before, all that "don't get involved". People participate. If it had been us by ourselves they would have evicted us ten times over, but it wasn't just us. There were [neighbourhood] assemblies and pensioners and neighbours. People are getting involved because they're fed up. Even if they don't get involved, just by the fact that they come and greet us, society is changing. Change is coming from below, which is slow, but it is accompanied by a great part of society.'[13]

The legal mechanisms used to grant workers' control have varied. The best arrangements for workers were achieved when they managed to lobby politicians to pass local laws allowing the municipalities to expropriate closed factories and donate them to the workers, that is, a definitive ruling giving over the machinery and other materials necessary for production to the newly-formed cooperative of workers. In most cases resolutions have not been so clearly in the workers' favour.

The most common arrangement has been for local government to provide a legal framework for a phased transfer to the workers, which leaves many options open to oust them. In these cases, expropriation has been approved as a temporary measure for two years, granting the use of the buildings needed to carry out the company's work in the form of a '*comodato*', a contract in which the council cedes the premises for free, on loan. If the temporary measure is agreed upon, the local government pays the rent on the premises and meets outstanding debts and compensation to the owner. After that time, the workers' cooperative has first option to buy the business.

From the point of view of local government, these arrangements are not an endorsement of socialism or Marxist theory, but a pragmatic attempt to contain social instability. Council officials have declared publicly that it is cheaper for the state to provide measures to continue production than to pay unemployment benefits or deal with the social implications of ever-increasing poverty. Ambivalence about the occupied factories is shown in the contradictory and chaotic legal framework used for them. This framework has been an exercise in hedging bets and hoping that the level of social need would recede so that things could go back to normal: bosses who own and workers who toil.

Workers have succeeded in making the majority of the recovered factories productive. This is an extraordinary achievement in the midst of Argentina's worst ever economic crisis, when credit has been non-existent since the end of 2001 and devaluation made imports unaffordable. As if that were not enough to contend with, owners were quitting or trying to liquidate sinking ships, not highly-profitable concerns, and in many cases had accumulated large debts. In those circumstances, making a business pay its way requires great skill and commitment as well as a tremendous amount of hard work.

When workers took control, unpaid bills meant many factories had no electricity or running water, never mind raw materials to produce or spare parts. In many cases, workers had to physically occupy the factory as it was clear the owners were trying to strip its assets, leading to confrontation and lengthy vigilance. In most cases state security forces intervened on behalf of the owners in a bid to evict the workers. The employees who managed to hold their ground invariably enjoyed, and needed, the support of a wide range of local people and organisations, whose demonstrations in some cases provided physical protection between factory and police.

A few factories have become emblematic of the movement, mostly through more intense media exposure, both traditional and alternative, and partly because they represent different approaches to what 'workers' control' can mean.

Zanon has become one of the best-known examples of workers taking charge of the means of production, and they are distinguished by a high level of support from their fellow citizens in the city of Neuquén, a thousand miles south of Buenos Aires. In 2000, the workers of one of the largest ceramic and tile factories in the country began to find themselves in constant conflict with management and the owners. During 20 years of functioning, conditions had been far from exemplary, but in the late 1990s they began to deteriorate badly. There were ten work-related deaths; salaries were cut, transport suspended (the factory is a few miles out of Neuquén) and the on-site first aid facilities withdrawn. The workers began to organise, first by displacing the corrupt leadership of their compliant trade union in 1998. By 2001, they were running the company.

Mr. Luiggi Zanon, the owner, was a 'model businessman' according to the province's governor. In 1999, Mr. Zanon decided that redundancies and salary cuts were the only way forward for his enterprise, and then he stopped paying salaries altogether. It was clear to all that he wanted to shut the factory down. The workers organised to resist the measures, using traditional pickets and roadblocks. When the owners tried to lock them out and sell off what remained, the workers locked themselves in – and found that many in Neuquén were willing to help them in the fight against paid heavies and police that looked the other way.

A battle of wills had begun. The courts ruled that the workers should be paid, and the owner responded by cutting off the gas supply. The workers made the ceramic ovens work for a day during their occupation and the owner sent 380 telegrammes sacking every one of them. The workers' legal advisor reckoned that was contempt of law, as a judge's ruling had ordered the re-opening of the plant as well as the payment of salaries due. On November 30th 2001 the situation exploded into street demonstrations and repression that left dozens injured. Popular support for the workers increased, and in response the police used tear gas around schools and hospitals as well as on the streets. In the weeks before the country exploded in the Argentinazo, Neuquén provided the supporting act for the people's rebellion that was to come.

By March 2002 the factory was working to full capacity once again. The 270 new owners got the factory back up to speed, even as they debated what to do and how to do it. In 2003 they continued to take on more employees, as orders were secured and production expanded.

Carlos Saavedra, coordinator at Zanon in 2003, talked to Esteban Magnani:

'I'm not an entrepreneur. I'm a worker and I want to give back to the community some of what it gave us. Here [in Zanon] nobody forgets the months we survived without producing thanks to the locals who buy 40,000 square metres a month of our production. The profits of the factory have to go to them. We want to solve the problem of unemployment and other social issues like health. As it grows this company will become more profitable. We got landed with a bit of a monster, without capital to invest, having to pay everything in advance. It's understandable that there wasn't much trust: Zanon owed a lot of money. He sank quite a few [of our suppliers]. The work of coordinating is a big responsibility. I don't control anyone and they are not on top of me. We simply all show what we've done. The numbers are clear. Anyone can see them. The fact that I'm the coordinator is up to the assembly. Every one has to fulfil the responsibility that is required of them.'[14]

Brukman is another factory in the limelight, this time because it failed to withstand repression by the police and judicial battering by the owners. Located in the heart of the city of Buenos Aires, this suit-making firm has become a symbol of the struggle for workers' control. In 2002 it became a site of contention between workers and capital, the latter on much better terms with the judiciary and with the police on their side. In the midst of a street battle which drew hundreds of policemen and thousands of demonstrators, the workers were evicted from their premises. Production moved to the streets, where the women and their sewing machines demonstrated their will to work.

Journalists Laura Vales and Sebastian Hacher followed the history and development of the Brukman recovery step by step:

'In December 2001 it was an almost abandoned factory. Its owners paid vouchers worth two pesos each week instead of wages. They didn't pay taxes or services such as electricity, water or gas. They did no maintenance and had debts twice the value of the factory. Two months later, when workers took over the place, the factory was filled with life. The business that seemed ruined had a lot to offer still: the workers got a wage, paid the services, and even some of the accumulated debts; they fixed the machines and paid the salary of a worker on sick leave. In April 2003, the factory had been run by the workers for 16 months. Then came the eviction. Behind the police appeared the owners reclaiming "their" property to "provide jobs".

Amalia, in her fifties, worked at Brukman since 1995. She's not sure, but around 1997 the problems started. "They gave us vouchers all the time, and we didn't even know what the daily rate was, and when we asked they said we owed them." The last two months under the owners were the hardest: "they gave us five pesos on Fridays, and all the time they pressed us to finish 1,000 suits so that they could get paid a cheque which never appeared".'

Not many of the over one hundred recovered factories bask

in much media coverage, although some of them make news for other reasons than their mode of management.

One of these has been Zanello, in Córdoba province, the only national tractor-maker. Its economic success and technical innovations (such as the first 'green' tractor that runs on natural gas) have brought it to the public eye. Only six months after being re-opened by the workers, Zanello dominated the internal market with 80 per cent of sales, presented four new models, and was planning an ambitious export campaign. For the 200-plus workers, such success was a world away from joining the ranks of the long-term unemployed. Zanello chose not to become a cooperative, but a limited company, with 33 per cent of control held by workers, 33 by management, 33 by the outlets that provided the capital for re-starting, and one per cent by the local government that passed the law to set it up. In 2003 it was given a national prize for innovation at the traditional rural business fair in Palermo, Buenos Aires, showing it is possible for recovered factories to do much more than survive.

In 2003 a range of occupied enterprises came together in a national meeting to discuss the advances and challenges they all face. The number of politicians who attended was notable, pointing to the degree to which recovering jobs has been a legal and political process. The problems raised by the workers were primarily about their factories' legal status, which for most remains precarious. Many of the recovered enterprises have reached the two-year limit for temporary expropriation and their future is by no means assured.

The other major challenge remains capital. The banking system had not provided credit since the crisis broke, so money is hard to come by. There are also clearly questions for potential investors as to whether worker-controlled enterprises should be supported at all. Given that larger business concerns are the ones that have the capital to invest and expropriation of private property is not something they take lightly, they are not natural allies. In fact, they are more likely to support sabotage of worker-run enterprises than their growth.

The main demands that came out of the national meeting were more definitive expropriations by the government, establishment of an investment fund, and a change in the Bankruptcy Law to enable workers to put a company back on its feet.

The very fact of having a tangible space and activity to defend makes recovered factories one of the most likely phenomena to endure, among the myriad social changes which have emerged since the 1990s in the midst of double-figure unemployment.

The middle class joins in

The Argentinazo cut across social class, as everyone except the very rich felt they had lost out. The losses were different, but the effect they caused was similar: outrage and fear for the future, a sense of being left defenceless in a hostile environment. A word that recurred in speeches and writing was *desamparo*, the feeling of being abandoned to fate.

Since the middle of the twentieth century until recently, the 'middle class' in Argentina has encompassed the largest proportion of the population. Perhaps many people's origins in immigration explains the generalised aspirations of most, who coined a widely-used refrain, the 'working middle class', to signal their belief in upward social mobility and their determination to be seen as middle class. The universal access to and quality of education meant that this dream was within the grasp of many, and the economic policies of state-led industrialisation and social rights in the 1950s and 1960s provided the means to achieve it.

Hence the shattering of their illusion of progress mobilised them as never before. Not surprisingly, the gap between their hopes and reality made them feel the loss of opportunities keenly. For the poorest below them, life has been an issue of survival for a long time and the state response has been violence and neglect for at least a generation. For the upper-middle class above them, there is always the option of leaving, one which thousands have chosen and many continue to consider – 80 per cent of those studying doctorates in 2003 said they were likely to go and stay abroad. Migration is not only restricted to the better-off, and in smaller proportion affects all layers of the middle classes.

The cacerolazos were seen as a predominantly middle-class affair in which once-affluent professionals took to the streets to protest against the initial restrictions and later freezing of their bank accounts. As ever, reality proved to be more complicated. The off-hand remark of the time to prove these protestors were only self-interested opportunists was 'they only march because they've touched their money,' and perhaps that was the reason of the moment. Certainly many of those who have fought against the corralito are far from radical. Yet their awareness of the need to participate in politics at large marks a change. They and many others were galvanised into action by having lost livelihoods, however unequal their incomes might have been.

For the left, political participation of the poorer sectors weighs much more heavily than the middle class waking up to the country's state of political disrepair. Yet middle and poorer sectors can help each other, and particularly during 2002, they did come together. In addition, although most MTDs provide political analysis and education for their members, it is also true than many join MTDs in order to access benefits and collaborate mainly with protests called to claim their rights from the state. So money, and livelihoods, are an important mobilising factor for everyone – including the extremely wealthy who fight for their interests with much greater success.

Accusations of self-interest could be levelled at anyone, and seem superfluous if those interests are realised in a collective and socially aware manner. It may not satisfy the radicals, but the move by the middle class from the sidelines into the thick of things improves the political culture of Argentina. Even among those who could ignore the crisis for longest, the middle class in work, changes in attitude can be perceived. The silence of the dictatorship had been transformed into the 'everyone for themselves' of the 1990s; poverty and unemployment were not understood as the results of state policies but as personal misfortune for which the victim was partly responsible. The movement from that individualism to the neighbourhood assemblies required both openness to change and the willingness to get involved in making change happen.

Practical solidarity has extended as different social sectors see that they are harmed by the same economic system. One example occurred when the shopkeepers who used to close their protective metal blinds during protests began to offer tea and sandwiches to piqueteros marching into the city. There is also a willingness to learn and support new initiatives, particularly those that confront the spectre of unemployment. That attitude can be felt when visiting a worker-occupied factory. The workers do a double shift: one manufacturing, the second receiving the academics, students, journalists, politicians and foreign activists who turn up at their door, asking questions and offering support. When trying to find out more about these social movements, one is struck by the wealth of writing on them (academic, activist and journalistic). The sheer volume of it suggests that there must be a clipboard-bearing researcher for every frontline activist in the country. What's more, some of it is carried by the mainstream media and considered 'news', underlining that the search for solutions extends far beyond those active in social changes.

The results of the 2003 election showed that some are still rich enough not to care – those who voted for Carlos Menem three times over, who still dream of cheap imports and foreign holidays. They were content to let the few at the top steal if necessary, as long as they got some of the booty. The very poor also made up the 20-odd per cent of votes he garnered, but their reasons were more complex. More important than the numbers, it is Menem's values that have been rejected by the population at large. 'Looking out for number one' is a familiar refrain in Argentina. Yet since the crisis in 2001, solidarity and the collective have become desirable values and therefore more possible. It may only be a few who participate daily in collective endeavours, but the example is noted and permeates mass forms of culture.

A crucial reason to consider the middle-class involvement in social changes is that they embody the regression of income and opportunity that has characterized the long Argentinian crisis. For most of the twentieth century social mobility created the largest middle class in Latin America and put the country at the top of social development in the region. The new poor have fallen from having jobs, businesses, houses, cars and education. Neo-liberalism showed that capitalism doesn't need as many workers, or even consumers, to turn profits for its international masters.

And when money became scarce, people began to find other resources.

Barter/Trueque

At the end of 1994 the economic model of one peso, one dollar and privatisations suffered a shock when capital suddenly took 'flight', although the full extent of the damage was not apparent immediately. The crisis that began in Mexico in 1995 spread in what became known as the 'tequila effect', which in Argentina meant that an estimated 20 per cent of available capital was whipped out of the country, leaving the economy in the lurch.

It was soon clear that unemployment was rising dramatically and the aspiring middle class, instead of advancing, was losing buying power. On the high street it translated into the mushrooming of loans, buying in instalments and with credit cards.

In the plazas and residential streets, it sparked off an idea. Two environmentalists had been trying out possible ways of creating a bartering system in their area, Bernal, in the province of Buenos Aires. On May 1st 1995, the first official 'node' of what became a network of barter clubs was inaugurated with two dozen neighbours on the premises of an old textile factory.

As there wasn't enough money to go round, Argentinians turned to a concept they have been familiar with over time: creating money and currencies as the occasion demanded. In the case of barter, the process arose from the people rather than the authorities and part of the idea was to get away from the values of capitalism and find social or alternative economic activities that would encourage solidarity and interaction in the local community. Soon people were trading everything from used appliances and clothing to dental care and haircuts, all for 'credits' used to purchase goods and services inside the barter system. In working-class neighbourhoods, foodstuffs were by far the preferred items.

The idea took off fast, and the number of nodes, as local barter sites were called, were hard to keep track of. Those participating grew exponentially. In six years over one million people were involved in *trueque* at more than 800 centres across the country. The annual circulation of credits was estimated at over US$1 billion. At their height, it was calculated that there were 6,000 barter clubs in the country. As the difficulties in making ends meet escalated towards the end of the long recession and after devaluation, need drove people in the millions to join a barter club. In the worst of the economic crisis during the early part of 2002, some six million Argentinians used barter as part of their survival strategies.

Conflict over how to manage the expansion resulted in splits among the coordinating groups and at least two important nation-wide groups emerged. The best-known national organisation was the Red Global del Trueque (Global Barter Network). It started up in 1995 and was overwhelmed by the numbers of people who tried to become members in 2002; the influx brought enough disruption to almost cause it to collapse. In some areas the Network estimated that 90 per cent of its 'currency' had been falsified. The organisers reported those accused of causing the problems, who were arrested. Now some nodes are still operating on a much smaller scale. Many of the sites active in 2003 are based in long-standing community centres which retained their credibility throughout.

The collapse of trueque as a mass phenomenon occurred in the second half of 2002. Theories abound as to why barter clubs imploded. Many have a ring of truth: the crisis brought many people who needed to buy but couldn't offer much and the sheer numbers made the system unmanageable. Others are partial truths which demonise the movement, the common refrain being that 'they were brought down by internal corruption.' A few took advantage of the system, but that is not the only reason for the collapse. The most dramatic claim is the one everyone seems to agree on: at a particular point in time all the clubs were flooded with false credits. These were well printed with expensive imported ink and paper and therefore pointed to a large organisation with resources, probably outside the system and possibly emanating from the shopkeepers and politicians who felt hard done by the barter.

During the growth years, though, the phenomenon had seemed unstoppable. It received state support, specifically from municipalities, on the basis that it provided a peaceful alternative to the social unrest expected given poverty levels and dismal prospects for the future. For commercial interests that suspiciously eyed the experiment as a threat to their business, barter was originally worth enduring because it served as a bridge between the formal and informal economies and helped move goods when consumption was low. Even government made the most of it, as in the town of Calchaquí in the province of Santa Fe, where the town council agreed to let its 13,000 inhabitants pay their local taxes with barter club credits.

A minority felt barter had the potential to move people beyond capitalism to a new understanding of trading based on exchange rather than profit, while most used it as a survival mechanism and considered it a temporary respite from untenable conditions. Yet the Argentinian experience is important because it involved so many people, proving that it is possible, at least temporarily, for economic systems to operate on principles other than profit.

Researcher Jeff Powell, who studied the barter phenomenon, suggests a number of reasons why it involved so many people. Clearly the long recession (technically a depression) and crisis played a part, as did Argentinians' particularly flexible view of currencies. Phenomena like changing national currencies and the experience of inflation that made the value of legal tender unreliable made it much easier for Argentinians to consider a new currency and a new economic system such as trueque. So, too, did the quasi-currencies issued by provincial governments and the monetary chaos that followed the corralito.

At that point, there was very little cash in circulation. Already before 2001, when provincial governments ran out of funds, they had paid their bills and salaries by issuing their own 'bonds', which quickly became accepted as alternative currencies in everyday use. Argentina reverted to a strange pre-capitalist state where barter and local currencies served the most immediate needs using values not recognised a few kilometres away. There were over a dozen of these informal currencies in circulation, including Lecops and Patacones, strange names redolent of Julio Cortázar's stories, even though they were mostly acronyms for bureaucratic jargon.[15]

Moreover, the social characteristics of the crisis were probably important. Most barter nodes emerged in lower-middle-class neighbourhoods where people had not only lost their jobs and incomes but also their security, the sense of having a future and the historic aspirations of improving one's lot. Gone were the real opportunities for social mobility and the progress felt from one generation to the next. Since the mid-1990s, instead of experiencing improvements, a large proportion of the population had to struggle daily to preserve what little they had, walking a knife-edge trying to not fall into the 'new poor'. Powell refers to studies worldwide that point to the adoption of alternative economic forms such as barter by the 'disenfranchised middle class'. People who have lost not only their income but also a way of fulfilling their aspirations through the formal economy.

At the height of trueque in 2002, journalist Mariana Iglesias wrote:

"'This system is not perfect, but it was a lifesaver for us," shared María Isabel Magarelli. She made lingerie and with it a good living. But then her husband lost his job and the recession meant sales dropped and she was persuaded to look into her nearest barter club. "I was studying Economics at the university and I really didn't believe the system could be viable. That's why I resisted getting involved. But the crisis forced me to leave my studies, we lost our family medical cover and the children had to change school. That's when I got involved with barter." At a node housed in an old factory, she and her husband sell lingerie and make between 600 and 700 credits per month. With those vouchers the family buys all the food they consume and the clothes they wear.

"'After selling my goods I exchange the credits for eggs, flour, shoes, t-shirts. And as I can't always find what I'm looking for, you become good at planning; when something unusual appears, you buy it and keep it," explains Isabel. Her three teenage children give her lists of what they want, and she tries to find everything. "I buy their school materials, their shoes and even the play station." She still sells her lingerie through the old distribution networks, and says, "I don't earn much that way, but they are the only real pesos coming in, so I use them to pay taxes." In her view, the system is not perfect, "because you often can't get what you want, but it is very practical and it feeds us. It was a real lifesaver".[16]

Neighbourhood assemblies

The massive cacerolazos of December 2001 contributed to the downfall of one president, and then another. The pot-banging protests of the following weeks and months also had concrete results: the spontaneous neighbourhood assemblies that sprang up around the city of Buenos Aires and beyond. They congregated in public spaces – on a street corner, in parks, or at the base of a monument – and provided a forum for anyone who wanted to participate and was assertive enough to get in line for the megaphone.

The sight of Argentinians coming together at street corners to talk about their problems might not seem so strange in a city with one of the world's greatest concentrations of psychologists and psychoanalysts – but it was, just because therapy is normally done on a one-to-one paying basis, and on the street it was free, in more than the monetary sense. It was group therapy via communal support, a cathartic outpouring of shared fears and frustrations. The move from the private sphere to the public broke down the isolation and fear felt by most, as they realised that they were not the only ones wondering what calamity would befall them next. The assemblies also fulfilled the collective and instinctive need for a forum for direct participation and involvement. The etymology of the word forum describes well the aims of the participants: an open exchange of ideas, an open space for debate, a court where justice is openly discussed. *Asambleas* were all of these things: a space for the people to re-take the power they had delegated to their political representatives, the practical extension of the chant 'que se vayan todos' and a chance to propose and debate what kind of country each wanted.

During the best part of 2002 assemblies brought together thousands of people across the country who debated not just what kind of a country to construct but also how to get there. Building on the way in which they congregated at street corners with their pots and pans ready to join others in protest, they soon found themselves engaged in long discussions and quickly fixed regular days and times to meet. Nobody asked them to turn up. They joined the ranks of the autoconvocados, those who have organised themselves. The unstructured nature of the original gatherings responded to the moment in which they arose, one of complete rejection of nearly every institution or organisation, even theoretically progressive forces such as left political parties. According to the think-tank Centro de Estudio Nueva Mayoría, there were at least 2,014 cacerolazos between December 19th 2001 and March of 2002. In that period over 200 assemblies came to life, and by August there were 329.

Much to the left's chagrin, the marching orders on politicians and politics as usual included them. Most of the (very small) left parties began to attend the assemblies and other new organisations in an effort to lead the masses of disgruntled voters towards revolution. But the people were unwilling to follow them. Although membership in these parties has benefited from the level of mobilisation since 2001, they continue to be divided by their fractious sectarianism, which they transposed onto the assemblies.

Many of the assemblies concluded quite quickly that they needed to join forces if their impact was going to be felt. To that end a weekly meeting of assembly representatives was agreed, called the *Interbarrial* (inter-neighbourhood), a multitudinous and vociferous gathering. Not far into its life, though, it encountered serious difficulties with activists from left parties, which were expressed in a spontaneous chant, '*respeten los mandatos, basta de aparatos.*' *Aparatos* is slang for political parties among other things, and people were saying, respect us, respect our desire to invent anew and stop your political games. Assembly members tried to reorganize the Interbarrial to sideline the extreme left parties, but these continued to wage their turf wars, leading to the fragmentation and stasis of the assembly movement, and the collapse of the Interbarrial. From the point of view of the left activists, asambleas were reinventing the wheel and going nowhere in their endless discussions.

Within individual assemblies discussion of national problems competed with talk of taking action to resolve local issues. In the capital's San Telmo neighbourhood, one assembly created a community garden and held a vaccination campaign for the cartoneros, those who live off picking cardboard out of the city's rubbish. In Belgrano, Flores, Villa Urquiza and numerous other neighbourhoods, the local assemblies have taken over vacant properties such as an abandoned bank branch, house, or corner bar to set up a soup kitchen and, in some instances, a community centre. At the Bar Alameda in Flores the local neighbourhood assembly runs a soup kitchen, sells used books at bargain prices and offers classes in everything from painting and pottery to yoga and improving self-esteem. Two additional neighbourhood assemblies in Flores occupied and took over an abandoned health clinic that, to their shock, was full of sophisticated, apparently useful medical equipment, and recruited some 60 local doctors to assist them in getting it going once again.

The assemblies grew dramatically within a few months, yet despite their achievements, a year on they were already on the wane. The reasons people gave for leaving were multiple: a reassessment of energy available for constant mobilisation; a sense that the assemblies were not leading anywhere because they had no clear aim; frustration with the political machinations, mainly of the far left parties; and a sense that they had fulfilled a valuable function in a moment of crisis, but that moment had passed.

A proportion of those involved in assemblies were keen to find other ways in which to make a political contribution, to participate and to oversee the politicians they so mistrusted. In some instances, the politicians themselves opened up new political spaces, particularly at the municipal level. Decentralisation and citizen oversight have been stated aims of many new legislative codes written in the 1990s, including the 1997 constitution of the newly-created administrative entity, the Autonomous City of Buenos Aires.

Yet it was only in 2002 that the city government encouraged citizens to become actively involved in decision-making through a process called participatory budgeting, which has been used successfully in countries like Brazil, Canada and South Africa. In Argentina it was a top-down political response to the upheavals of 2001.

Anthropologist Dennis Rodgers spent time in 2003 looking at the impact of this new initiative. Although the idea came from politicians, people have grasped the opportunity and many thousands are participating in planning how to allocate city funds. Neighbourhood groups are coordinated by the decentralisation department of the city government. They discuss priorities for their area and vote on how to order the actions, which are then fed back to the central authorities. A council of locally-elected representatives oversees the final decisions made at legislative level. The web site of the government of Buenos Aires was proud to announce that of the 338 neighbourhood priorities voted in 2002, more than 80 per cent were completed or in the process of being finalised.[17] Rodgers reports that the process was less bureaucratic than the famous case of Porto Alegre, Brazil, and that it seemed to be generating a genuine sense of power in the local community.

The fact that the government called the local budget meetings 'neighbourhood assemblies' shows that it seeks to inherit, if not co-opt, the political capital of the rambling assemblies that took over street corners for much of 2002. Critics point out that so far only miniscule portions of the budget have been up for discussion (only two per cent for the 2003 budget) and that organisational problems such as poor information about the time and place of meetings hampered participation. Also, the process was not legislated but rather created by decree, making it vulnerable to cancellation after the next change in government. In any case, the 'official' assemblies appear to be a forum for many, even as the original neighbour-hood assemblies continue to work on their own political development and try to find the best way to engage with the continuing difficulties faced by many.

The legal route

Since 2002, the financial centre of Buenos Aires has sported extensive façades of metal sheeting, covering the doors and windows of banks, which are all grand buildings, making the city look post-apocalyptic. The metal is ugly and plain, and closer inspection shows thousands of indents, as though a meteorite rain had hailed on them. They were bent, but not pried open, by the anger of thousands of savers who found that their money was taken from them.

Capitalism rules, but when the going got tough, private property was not sacred. As ever, it was only the property of those least able to flee which was affected – the rich had long taken their money well beyond the metal walls thrown up to protect the glass and marble banks. Within days of Domingo Cavallo's December 1st 2001 announcement of his last-ditch restrictions, injunctions were being lodged in the courts to contest the corralito's constitutionality. By the end of the week over 200 cases had been brought before judges. By the new year Eduardo Duhalde was in office and one of his first actions was to revoke convertibility. He then went on to decree the corralón, freezing accounts and decreeing their value. One peso was no longer worth one dollar and nobody really knew what would happen next.

Many people thought that once they could access their bank accounts again, everything would be fine, no matter what the peso did. It was clear the peso would be devalued; nobody knew by how much, but people felt safe in the knowledge that their deposits were made *in U.S. dollars.* Some 70 per cent of all accounts in the banking system were held in dollars. The majority of savers had chosen to keep their foreign currency in foreign banks in Argentina on the assumption that those entities could not go bankrupt and their international status would protect their clients from government actions.

The misplaced trust of savers was about to be shattered. By government decree all accounts, still frozen, were forcibly converted to pesos. The official exchange rate for the conversion was set at 1.4 pesos to the dollar and maintained as long as possible. But within weeks the 'real' floating rate was beginning to edge up, reaching two pesos by March and almost four pesos to one dollar in June. The forced conversion meant that the 1,500 pesos that could be withdrawn per month (up from 1,000 pesos initially) had lost half their value in March and were only worth a quarter of their original value by June. Economic measures were dreamt up and announced day by day, and the population lived in fear of what might come next. Nobody paid anything, waiting for the chaos to abate. And people soon found themselves literally banging at the doors of their banks demanding their money be returned. Then savers took their fight to the streets, to the media, to the internet and to the courts.

By April 2002, over 210,000 injunctions had been made against the corralito and corralón in the federal justice system alone, and more were requested at the provincial level. They represent only a small fraction of the nine million savers in the financial system, but they created enough critical mass to bring out warnings of monetary meltdown if they achieved their purpose to the detriment of everyone else.[18]

The protests took place very much within the context of capitalist expectations: the main argument in the injunctions was the violation of the constitutional right to property. More than half of the claims were successful, although the results were down to each court and judge. Although their claims were taken up in several Supreme Court rulings, the overall effect was piecemeal success with no comprehensive agreement to repeal the decrees which brought the corralón into being.

The protesters were a mixed bag politically and in many cases were pitting themselves against political power for the first time. They began their cases as individuals with a claim, and they ended up creating large networks of organised protest. The way the legal system works – slowly, requiring attendance over time – fomented the commitment of thousands of citizens to protest government policy. As cacerolazos became fewer and demonstrations smaller, an increasing number of people took recourse to the courts and banded together with others in the same situation: exchanging information, sharing tips and forming alliances. A new term and social actor were born: '*ahorristas*', or 'savers'.

There were some swings and roundabouts in the economic measures dreamed up by the government during 2002. The first set of decrees included a clause that forced banks to convert debts contracted in dollars to pesos on a one-to-one basis. This meant that the vast credit contracted during the 1990s suddenly lost at least a third of its value, making repayment a lot easier. The measure had been lobbied for by big business (the Clarín group, owner of the largest newspaper in the country, was notoriously indebted and vocal). In terms of the number of people, the conversion benefited individuals with debt or mortgages most, but in terms of money, businesses saw the greatest benefit. But even for those whose debts became 'pesified', the even greater shrinkage of their income in the aftermath of the crisis meant debts stretching out over much longer periods of time.

All in all, legal wrangles over money were reserved for those with the resources to make a claim. Yet the legal path to redress from an overbearing state had been pioneered by the human rights movement, and gave citizens new political tools.

Loud and clear

The year of hitting rock bottom economically, 2002. Cash was in short supply and prospects were bleak. Still, the theatres were full and the number of shows impressive. Festivals proliferated – dance, film, music – and they were all packed. It could have been escapism, as there was certainly much to forget, but somehow most of it wasn't. The content was political, a lot of events were free or almost, sliding scales for tickets made an appearance and the resurgence of solidarity meant performances took place everywhere from grand theatres to factories and shantytown squares. Argentinians and foreigners alike remarked bemusedly at the quality and diversity of cultural offerings available throughout the crisis.

One of the positive legacies of the convertibility years was the access it gave young and old to computer and film equipment. Cameras, software and access to the internet all became more affordable with a peso worth a dollar, making foreign goods easier to acquire. When the peso fell to a more real value, many still had the tools with which to communicate, and that is just what they did. The internet became a much-used organising tool for many of the urban (and better off) activists. The number of sites relating to the crisis and people's responses proliferated. Many were windows to the world where everyone could air their frustration and anger. Web access was not as exclusive as might have appeared, as internet cafes were (and continue to be) ubiquitous and in constant use in poorer parts of the cities. The large numbers of Argentinians living abroad also contributed to making the internet an important channel of communication.

For some burgeoning projects, the Argentinazo provided the push from the margins into the centre. The international Indymedia network of alternative, grassroots news activism had begun to organise in the country in 2000. As one of the founders in Argentina, Sebastian Hacher, put it, 'in 2000 there were two of us, now we get 10,000 hits a day.' In 2001 it became the best and sometimes only source of news about what people were really doing. The news service is staffed entirely by volunteers, who finance their time and equipment themselves.

Many new groups had the Argentinazo to thank as the catalyst that brought them together. An example is Argentina Arde (Argentina Burns), another 'counter information' collective which aims to make public the events and people the mainstream media ignore. They use writing, photos and video to be part of events and contribute to the record being kept for posterity.

And they are not alone. When Indymedia called for a gathering of alternative media during 2002, over 200 people turned up – activists, journalists, photographers and film-makers. Unity was suggested but impossible, but collaboration does take place and a range of collective efforts have led to an array of books, films, papers and magazines. Their work was crucial for many Argentinians outside the country, and also for those inside when sources of news became very selective in their coverage. One of the cacerolazos in February 2002 was organised primarily to protest against the news blackout exercised by the main dailies, which suddenly refused to report on the demonstrations taking place weekly. Social unrest had mysteriously ceased to be news, a clear attempt to curtail participation.

The revolution in accessibility to film and editing equipment meant the emergence of a generation who use documentaries as their means of protest and proposal. Hand-held cameras have facilitated footage of every major social upheaval, while the low production costs for a video cassette have made distribution possible far and wide.

The greatest growth area has been in politically-engaged documentaries, a stance known across Latin America as *compro-metido* (committed). There are films of piquetes and police repression, of the violent clashes on the 19th and 20th, of neighbourhood assemblies and worker-run factories. The frames shot have been made into films which have been shown to thousands in festivals and screenings in Argentina, and many have made it abroad. International attention and solidarity has seen foreign directors make their way to shoot their own takes on the situation, and also to collaborate with national directors and crews.

One of the number of associations of filmmakers is the Grupo de Cine Insurgente (Insurgent Cinema Group) that came together to enable the production and distribution of films with social content. The Group inherited a rich history of politically-engaged cinema in Argentina, such as the Grassroots Cinema founded by Raymundo Gleyzer. The quality of Argentinian feature cinema in the 1990s had already been evidenced by the number of films that made it to commercial distribution in Europe, even in the UK, where Argentine cinema was almost unheard of. Engaging thrillers like 'Nine Queens' seemed far removed from politics, but other successes like 'Crane World', a grainy black and white view at the life of a middle-aged, unemployed worker trying to make ends meet, brought social reality to the art house.

Purchasing books is a national passion which can still be indulged in central Buenos Aires. Even as the cinemas were full, publishing almost ground to a halt between 2001 and 2002 and book buying waned. Foreign investment dried up, affecting the larger publishers with international connections. Smaller, local firms were affected by lack of income and the expense of basic materials like paper. Devaluation of the peso meant everything became much more expensive, and if it was imported, unavailable or prohibitive. But the bookshops somehow managed to be full of new titles and sales happened, a near miracle.

The less money there was to go around, the more vibrant and original artistic expression seemed to be, and much of it interacted directly with the political problems and events, as they affected everyone. Protests like the escraches described at the beginning of the chapter returned to form, becoming more thought provoking, more creative in the ways in which they aimed to raise consciousness.

Other manifestations engaged with grief, death and political violence. Some escraches were known for their original 'road signs', none of them from the highway code. They come courtesy of the Grupo de Arte Callejero (Art on the Streets), a collective that has taken part in protests organised by HIJOS, and exhibited at the 50th Venice Biennal in 2003. Their work entitled Cartography of Control included a map of Buenos Aires with circles identifying centres of economic power, and places of military repression, conflicts and military installations. The Group was also responsible for the memorials made to mark the deaths of civilians at the hands of state repression on December 20th 2001.

It appeared to some a strange response to crisis, but the urge to express what was felt and thought seemed to become imperative. A young novelist who teaches creative writing, José María Brindisi, remarked on how surprised he was to see the demand for his classes rise to capacity in 2002, after a few lean years when the lack of spare cash appeared to stifle creative undertakings.

But wit and humour and cutting commentary were not limited to those with the resources to film, or write, or have a website. Graffiti became a powerful tool in expressing social unrest and covered many available spaces. Much was angry and to the point, but some captured the truth in poetic ways that have stayed in people's minds. An informal survey throws up as the most memorable: 'they piss on us and the press say it's raining.'

International solidarity

The global media showed images of supermarkets being looted, of the angry crowds in the Plaza de Mayo as the helicopter whisked de la Rúa away from the presidency, of savers doorstepping their banks. The most disturbing and sensationalist images were those of people fighting over pieces of meat cut from live cows after a truck carrying cattle was overturned. In a country with two heads of cattle per inhabitant, where beef had been part of the staple diet, these images invoked revulsion and disbelief across the world. The focus of the media left most of the picture out of the frame.

Meanwhile, very different stories were breaking through the internet, providing another vision of events. The cacerolazos, the burgeoning assemblies, the suddenly-discovered piquetes and barter clubs sent a loud buzz through international networks of activists. The creative and articulate powers of communication of Argentinians impressed those who had no knowledge of the country.

Soon many were going and seeing for themselves. As John Jordan, an experienced participant of the global anti-capitalist movement, put it:

"'We know what they are against, but what do they want?' I was tired of hearing this refrain, targeted at the global anti-capitalist movements. We knew what we wanted: another kind of globalisation, where life comes before money, where direct democracy and ecological sustainability become the norm, where progress is defined by the amount of diversity and dignity in the world, rather than the amount of cash that changes hands. The problem was that we didn't know how to get it. Many of us realised that, however many economic summits we protested against or GM crops we uprooted, we weren't really bringing the new worlds we were dreaming of any closer.

In early 2002, while the movements were trying to come to terms with the fear and uncertainty caused by September 11 and the war on terror, something happened that no one expected. Through the movements' emails, websites and face-to-face gatherings, stories emerged of a land where politicians were so discredited that they were ridiculed wherever they went, angry middle-class women smashed up banks, occupied factories were run by their workers, ordinary people held meetings to decide how to run their neighbourhoods, and thousands of unemployed people blocked highways, demanding food and jobs. It sounded like France in 1968 or Spain during the civil war, and yet it was lasting for months across a country 11 times the size of the UK, in a state that was recently one of the world's top 20 strongest economies, a sparkling model of emerging markets, the most compliant pupil of the International Monetary Fund, with a capital city known as the 'Paris of Latin America'. It was happening in Argentina.

I had always wondered what a real grassroots rebellion would look like, how it would feel, what it would smell like. I had imagined huge crowds spontaneously taking to the streets, the smell of teargas drifting across barricades, the noise of hundreds of thousands of voices calling for a new world as the government fled from office and people took control of their everyday lives. All of these things have happened in Argentina over the past year, inspiring activists from as far afield as South Africa, Italy, Thailand and Belgium to visit and see how a crippling economic tragedy was being transformed into an extraordinary laboratory for creating alternative economic models, to witness the reinvention of politics from the bottom up.'[19]

Argentina appeared out of nowhere on the international stage of the resistance to neo-liberalism, but it certainly made a splash. Participants in the international movement searching for the possibility of a better world found the novel initiatives taken in Argentina hugely inspiring, and at the same time, by travelling there, reminded Argentinians that they belonged to a wider reality affecting their continent and the world. The international presence was felt strongly among the most dynamic of the new social forms of action, even as it was allowed to pass under the radar of the mass media and therefore public opinion. And the idealism which fuelled the interest became a network of international solidarity that keeps growing.

The international interest has also cross-fertilized with Argentinians who have made their home across the five continents and have felt the need to contribute something from afar. In many European countries, for example, there had been no people-to-people political exchange since the dictatorship, but in 2002 those networks of solidarity became live once more.

Notes

1 López Echagüe, H. *La política está en otra parte, viaje al interior de los nuevos movimientos sociales* Buenos Aires, Norma, p. 34

2 See http://www.infored.org.ar/VerArticulo.aspx?IdArticulo=1877

3 Farmelo, M. 'Gender Dynamics Among the Organized Unemployed: "We are not *Piqueteros*,"' Hanover, *ICWA Letters*, August 2002

4 *Clarín* special report on piqueteros, http://www.clarin.com/diario/especiales/piqueteros/

5 Farmelo, op. cit.

6 For a detailed account of the events of June 1996 see 'La vida en un piquete. biografía y protesta en el sur argentino' by Javier Auyero, available on-line at http://www.sunysb.edu/sociology/faculty/Auyero/vidaenpiquete.htm

7 Although splits in Aníbal Verón began to take place in 2003

8 López Echagüe, op. cit. pp. 68–9

9 Ibid. p.19

10 Ibid.

11 See http://www.crisisstates.com/CAW/index.htm

12 See http://www.argentina.indymedia.org/news/2003/08/124985.php

13 *Ocupar, Resistir, Producir,* Movimiento Nacional de Empresas Recuperadas, No.1, November 30 2002

14 Magnani, E. *El Cambio Silencioso*, forthcoming 2004, Buenos Aires, Prometeo

15 Lecops: *Letras de Cancelación de Obligaciones Provinciales*, and Patacones, the name given to *Letras de Tesorería para la Cancelación de Obligaciones emitidas por la Provincia de Buenos Aires,* taken from the name for money used by Patoruzú, a local comic strip character

16 Iglesias, Mariana, 'Con el trueque ya se compran campos, autos y hasta casas,' *Clarín*, February 14 2002

17 See http://www.buenosaires.gov.ar/pp/

18 Smulovitz, C. 2003 'Protest by other means: legal mobilizations in the Argentinian crisis', paper presented at the conference Rethinking Dual Transitions, March 2003, Harvard University. See http://www.wcfia.harvard.edu/conferences/argentinepolitics/papers.asp

19 'Out of the Ordinary,' *The Guardian*, January 25 2003

Conclusions

Crisis and opportunity

The crisis of 2001 brought out the best in Argentinians and as a collective they achieved tremendous things. They began by providing the pressure to unseat a president or two and continued via myriad forms of involvement in social and political change. Before 2001 there was no precedent for people reclaiming their rightful power over the political process, across class and political divides – particularly those people not already organised. Paradoxically, people have held on to the feeling that things could not get any worse as a reason to go out and make them better. Hence a sense of potential improvement.

Yet looking back from the limited vantage point of two years, it is easy to maintain that nothing much has changed. There is a Peronist president and the economic model remains in place even while unemployment and poverty continue to soar. It is much harder to hold now that the people announced a new era with the steady rhythm of their pots and pans. They may have voiced the need for a profound institutional transformation in politics and the economy, but no new solutions have emerged.

So in 2003 the question on everyone's lips is 'to what extent has anything really changed – politics been renewed, the economy been turned around?' The biggest change is that possible answers now have to take into account a population much more engaged with power, even if the political system remains standing. Outside Argentina the questions are slightly different: 'will this lead to a new party, a new political system, a new way of dealing with power at the state level?' In the short term, these are the wrong questions. To those who hope change will come from the new social movements, the answer is that these groups are not interested in taking over the state.

As for the left-wing parties, even though it is their aim to take the state, they lack the political skills and support to do so. The many and sectarian left parties do not speak for the masses. Their impact has been contradictory, as they have supported social mobilisation and been invigorated by the protests, yet at the same time served as a brake on activism. Argentina's left-wing and progressive social change organisations share a divisiveness common to them all; the few exceptions meet resistance to calls for unity. Although between them they do bring together a respectable slice of the electorate, they fail to either make it big individually or come together to share their votes. Moreover, President Kirchner has successfully occupied part of the political space traditionally held by the left, further weakening their appeal.

The real answer to the question of the depth and permanence of change requires taking a step back and seeing the enormous creativity of social responses in the context of the many possible ways in which societies deal with devastating circumstances. In this sense, the answers lie in seeing not only what happened, but also what didn't.

Economic hardship and social chaos lead more predictably to violence and repressive measures that promise 'social order', rather than to solidarity. Given Argentina's militarised and right-wing past it is remarkable how far the military was from the action in 2001. Furthermore, we would expect social anxiety and insecurity to lead to atomising responses, paranoia, social polarisation and confrontation – an all against all. Instead, the opposite occurred. Solidarity is back in fashion and the optimistic speak of a cultural change.

Given Argentina's history, it would also seem likely that instability would encourage the appearance of a 'strong leader', of order kept with the benefit of force. After a century of saviours of the fatherland (including Perón), in times of crisis Argentinians have turned to strongmen to deliver the glorious destiny to which they have aspired. Politics in the twentieth century were dominated by men who offered progress through order imposed by military governments, or that provided people a role in the social hierarchy where everyone was recompensed for knowing their place, as with Perón.

Even at the end of the last dictatorship, it took the military's own disarray and their rout in the Malvinas/Falklands war in 1982 before their 'saving the nation' mission could be ousted. Change could be glimpsed when the threats to democracy from the military galvanised society onto the streets by the millions to support President Alfonsín in 1987. Yet hyperinflationary chaos led straight back to voting in another 'tough guy', Carlos Menem, who came to rescue the country with his disciplining neo-liberalism. The 'father figure' – the protector, the provider – is a strong motif in Argentinian politics, present also in the everyday ways in which votes are really won.

The social disintegration of Argentina's recent collapse would seem more fertile ground for demagogic populism and the outward violence of finding a scapegoat than the peaceful mass mobilisation it inspired in reality. 'Que se vayan todos' was partly about giving up on the idea of a saviour, and one of the most powerful shared perceptions which emerged out of the Argentinazo was that of the ordinary citizen as an heroic figure.

A recurring metaphor used since the Argentinazo is that the people, collectively, have grown up and out of needing a father to guide them. The superhuman father figure who was supposed to have all the virtues of the collective and none of the shortcomings was a fiction which allowed Argentinians to avoid taking responsibility for their own destiny. The pressures of 2001 may have marked a political coming of age where the need for collective effort has replaced the search for a saviour.

Instead of Argentinians seeking a leader who can take care of them, the search is on for ways in which people can help themselves and others.

The power of old habits does not wane overnight, though. Powerful men retain an important place in politics and haven't gone away, but have simply moved back from the limelight. The best example could be former president Eduardo Duhalde, who remains the most powerful fixer in Peronism (and the PJ the only political party with mass following).

A force stronger than habit also works against change: fear. A sense of insecurity pervades everyday conversations and is fanned by the media. So although crime has not risen dramatically since 2001, the level of perceived insecurity has. Crime still affects predominately poor neighbourhoods, but the middle classes get the press coverage when crimes occur to them.

But even responses to insecurity have changed. To prevent muggings of school children, communities have teamed up to provide 'safe passage' through marked streets where neighbours, shopkeepers and schools make sure the children are safe and have somewhere to run to for help. This began as one neighbourhood initiative, but the example has been taken up more widely. They call the project 'security is solidarity' and it arises from a much more sophisticated concept of security than the repressive rhetoric Argentina is used to. Even if actions are limited in scope, the collective efforts to face harsh realities have generally been inspired and innovative.

One method shared by many social groups to combat fear and fixed mindsets has been the 'assembly', the gathering of equals to discuss and agree ways forward. As Andrés Fernández of the MTD Solano said in an interview, 'we don't believe that there should be an enlightened one who knows what the answers are, what is the way. Knowledge is part of what we are, "one can't know everything, only between us can we know" as the Zapatistas say.'[1] The insistence across neighbourhood assemblies, in piquetero groups, and in the recovered factories, is that discussion among equals is the only way to build the country anew.

No more wholesale delegation of power to those who promise salvation, because they don't deliver. The talk on the factory floor and in the streets has been about power and counterpower, checks and balances. People are 'doing it for themselves' but also, for the first time, it seems, they are holding a collective debate on the nuts and bolts of power: what it is, who has it, how to wield it, how to resist it – the beginnings of a more sophisticated, shared understanding of how power works. The 'us and them' of politicians and people had allowed the ruled to disassociate themselves from the decisions taken in their name. But the crisis of representation brought them up sharply against the fact that these awful, corrupt politicians had been voted in, even though their dirty deals had been common knowledge.

The ability to analyse and organise were not new, of course; there were myriad social forces predating the 'new' forms of organisation described in the previous chapter. These new shoots have long roots and so are unlikely to wither rapidly, even if they mutate over time.

In the process of briefly reviewing the failings of Menem's neo-liberal agenda, it is easy to forget that there was much else going on, both in society and in politics. Menem's neo-liberal hegemony was real but it was not uncontested, and he cannot be blamed for the driving need felt by broad sectors of the population for stability at any price, or worse, for another stab at the 'greatness' the country had always felt entitled to. Argentinians' wishful thinking transformed the shallow flattery of interested parties into the belief that Argentina was one among the rich nations.

As more and more Argentinians acknowledged their self-deception, the ground was prepared for the sense of betrayal and anger expressed by most in December 2001. Social mobilisation was built on the disappointing experience of decades, as though December 2001 had been the last straw which convinced many that the way they had been heading for years was taking them nowhere, fast.

Reasons to believe that long-term changes might come from the crisis of 2001 can be found in the social responses to some of the most extreme and difficult circumstances faced by Argentina in the last 30 years. The last military dictatorship, with its totalitarian and divisive social and economic policies, generated a reaction in society that leaves the military no political place, after over 50 years of intermittent rule. Moreover, the persevering work of 'memory' of the crimes of the dictatorship and the defence of human rights has aided the development of citizens who are much more aware of their relation to the state. State repression undoubtedly highlighted the rights citizens have in relation to the state, while citizens' responsibilities have historically been shunned, exemplified in pervasive tax evasion. The crisis of 2001 brought home the fact that rights and responsibilities go together. In a more practical sense, the deep economic crisis of 1989 served as the catalyst for the creation of a wide range of social and political endeavours during the 1990s, and after 2001 a new wave of initiatives was activated.

In sum, after the dictatorship came the social realisation of the value of democracy; after 1989 came the awareness that economic success is not measured only by growth figures, but also by levels of employment and social cohesion. It may be that 2001 was the moment for society to tackle the political system, to be aware that without checks, it is not even properly representative.

The latest crisis appears to be leading to a consciousness that participation in power is the way forward. It is too early to say how this understanding will be realised over time. Social scientists, journalists and activists are hard at work to document the changes in individuals' 'sense of their own subjectivity', a term used as often by piqueteros as by academics, to see if how they understand social processes and their role in politics has truly changed.

What will Argentinians do with this new consciousness? The impressive sophistication of the discourse across all organisations and commentators doesn't always seem to impact on action, and not all actions make a difference. But both groups and the individuals within them share characteristics that have the potential to shift social dynamics profoundly: an insistence on equality, the rejection of hierarchies and authoritarianism, and an understanding that the future is not up to the rulers of Argentina, but to every single soul who wants to call it home.

The recent history of how society has responded to crises provides hopeful antecedents. Results are not instantaneous, but in time, they become ever more concrete. The events of 2001 appear to have that type of transformative power, but much more time is needed to assess their impact. Judging by their actions, Argentinians appear to have reached a collective conclusion that blaming the government is not the answer. Their actions say that the political system they have, as flawed as any representative democracy, is usable. But they have to use it – or lose it, as they did to military dictatorships and corrupt civilian elites throughout the twentieth century.

Note

1   See   http://www.solano.mtd.org.ar/article.php3?id_article=16

Postscript

'We are all sons and daughters of the Madres and Abuelas de Plaza de Mayo'
From President Kirchner's speech to the United Nations General Assembly in September 2003

The Kirchner factor

Restructuring the high echelons of the military; devising controls on capital; implementing a court to deal with (large scale) tax evasion; confronting corruption in the police; suspending senior police and prison service officials; pressuring the Congress to impeach corrupt Supreme Court judges and annul the amnesty laws of Punto Final and Obediencia Debida, berating the economic establishment regarding their lack of commitment to the nation; granting audiences to social movements from the Madres to the piqueteros; standing up to the IMF and not accepting every single one of its conditions.

This sounds like an agenda dreamt up by progressives around a late-night dinner table, when the wine flows and the conversation turns to changing the world. Yet the list includes only the most salient decisions taken by President Néstor Kirchner, who reached power in May 2003. His actions were soon dubbed 'the K effect'. His attitudes have been utterly unexpected and so, too, people's response to them. From the day he was sworn in all through his first 100 days of government, the most common reply to the question 'what do you make of him?' was 'I'm hopeful'. Hopeful seemed about as optimistic as Argentinians were willing to admit to, as the economic situation continued to bite. Hopeful may appear lukewarm, but hope is a powerful feeling to arouse.

As the political system lost legitimacy toward the end of the 1990s, the electoral abstention rate climbed ever higher. There were widespread expectations during 2002 that a terminal lack of participation in the formal political process would make the threat of 'que se vayan todos' a reality at the ballot box.

It was not to be the political will of the majority. By the time the elections came round in April 2003, 77 per cent of the population turned out to vote despite the continuing cacerolazos, the new networks created between middle and working class activists, and their generalised calls for abstention. It was an exercise in pragmatism, making do with the least worst option. Until the last minute, Menem dominated the news as the frontrunner and although at the time Kirchner did not represent a positive alternative, he was better than the nasty medicine on offer from the surgeon who had almost bled them to death. Menem was not being coy in his campaign. He promised 'to bring out the military onto the streets to stop social chaos,' and to clean the streets of 'Marxists and delinquents'.

Menem won the first round of the presidential elections, albeit narrowly, showing that magical thinking remains a factor in Argentinian politics – inherent in the 'logic' he touted and others repeated, 'he got us into this mess, only he can get us out.' Kirchner came second, but was predicted 60 to 70 per cent success in the second round from which Menem then withdrew, causing maximum political damage to his opponent. The candidate who came in third, Ricardo López Murphy, originated from the UCR, but the party he founded was significantly right of centre. Elisa Carrió came in fourth, also a UCR dissident, this time on the left, also leading her own party, ARI. The UCR gave an historic worst performance when Leopoldo Moreau took 2.3 per cent of the votes.

That Néstor Kirchner, an unknown quantity in national politics, reached the presidency, was mostly the result of the internecine quarrels within Peronism. The PJ failed to agree on a single presidential candidate, and so ran three. Then-President Duhalde threw his considerable weight behind Kirchner, and for the duration of the campaign the new man did little to come out of Duhalde's shadow. His lack of charisma and avoidance of electoral marketing kept him a bit of a mystery, or even better, not much like any other politician. And in 2003 in Argentina, that turned out to be an advantage. Commentator Artemio López summed it up: 'his figure is of the anti-hero, and in that sense, it is a positive attribute.' He was, in short, seen as an outsider, and one with little power base of his own and therefore institutionally weak, in spite of his Peronist credentials.

The expectations everyone had of this political unknown were so low that in the first instance, his actions evoked surprise and even suspicion. The disenchantment with politicians felt across society made people wary of any initiative, waiting to see when self-interest would came into play. Yet for many, the worst he's done in the first few months of government is be personally involved in many matters, revealing a tendency to want to control everything and personalism is a recurring trait in Argentinian politics.

A lawyer by training, Kirchner had been governor of the sparsely-populated province of Santa Cruz, in the Patagonian south, rich in oil. He had belonged to the Peronist movement since his student days when he was involved with the Juventud Peronista, a left-wing youth organisation with membership overlap with the Peronist guerrilla groups, although it appears Kirchner's militancy never crossed over to armed struggle. Kirchner and his wife, Senator Cristina Fernández, lived in Santa Cruz during those years and almost nothing is known about them in that time, including why they escaped the ubiquitous repression. Their friends and relatives have been unusually loyal and not a whiff of scandal has ever attached itself to them.

Cristina Fernández has kept a relative low profile since her husband became president, surprising political commentators, though she is one of his key advisors. As a deputy and then senator in Congress, she enjoyed a higher national profile than he through the 1990s. Her rhetoric, specially since Kirchner's ascent to power, is old-fashioned left Peronist. In an interview with the main daily *Clarín* she said a number of things normally associated with the left or NGOs:

'The military coup of 1976 found an Argentina where workers participated in almost 50 per cent of the country's GDP. Today that participation is not even 30 per cent. The final chapter of the tragedy was Menem, who did things even the military didn't dare do. That's why Argentina's great challenge, as well as economic and social, is moral and cultural. The commitment to what happens to one's fellow citizens or what happens to the country was finished off by the terrible and savage repression we had in 1976. Beyond the mistakes of the '70s generation, which were many, repression created the idea that to put yourself on the line for what you think is bad, brings problems and it is better to keep yourself to yourself, not get involved.'[1]

Kirchner has made much of having stayed true to his convictions. It is known he doesn't like being crossed, and can lash out when he is, which he proved once in the Casa Rosada by publicly snubbing his vice-president Daniel Scioli after he made remarks contradicting government policy. On becoming president he declared his worldly goods, the bulk of which were acquired before he entered politics. He owns considerable property, but his two cars are both Hondas, not quite in the same Ferrari-driving league in which Menem liked to be seen. Yet in some ways their success has more similarities than differences. Both ably captured the collective mood of the moment, Menem by providing stability – no matter how precarious – entertainment, easy credit and international recognition. For Kirchner, the demands were radically altered: a departure from politics as usual, honesty, a willingness to listen to people and rule with them, not over them. And he has been delivering, in many ways, over and beyond the expectations anyone had of a career Peronist politician.

Kirchner has been bold where he could expend little political capital for good returns: beheading the high command of the armed forces in his first week in office or standing up to the bullying of the corrupt Supreme Court. He has also made the most of popular feeling and the tremendous approval ratings, which have ranged between 70 and 90 per cent in his first 100 days, an unheard of show of public support. He has used it, for example, to tackle police crimes and corruption, a hornets' nest of state complicities with terrorism, organised crime and repression; his willingness to accuse chiefs of police is perhaps the most telling indicator that he may have no dirty secrets himself.

The president's vigour in tackling impunity also owes much to his ability to take advantage of his public mandate. In July 2003, when Spanish judge Baltazar Garzón demanded the extradition of members of the military involved in human rights abuses, Kirchner revoked the standing presidential decree that had made extradition impossible. This measure was only approved once he could be reasonably certain that the wheels were in motion to try those responsible in Argentina. Hence the initiative to put through parliament Argentina's adherence to international law in relation to crimes against humanity, and the weight behind the process to annul the laws of Punto Final and Obediencia Debida.

The battle of wills that gained him most recognition has been with the IMF. The negotiations had been going on for months, but in early September 2003, Kirchner refused to use Argentina's reserves to pay the Fund. As *The Economist* put it, 'after missing a [US]$2.9 billion payment to the International Monetary Fund on September 9th, [Argentina] distinguished itself with the single largest non-payment of a loan in the Fund's history.'[2]

The IMF was pushing for its usual recipe of austerity measures and it was told in no uncertain terms that austerity had taken Argentina to depression and disaster before, so why make the same mistake again? Yet while the agreement Kirchner signed has been heralded as a victory over the IMF, it contains conditions that prioritise payment of international debt and impede economic recovery.

The Fund was vocal in its advocacy of private (privatised) interests, demanding rises in tariffs of public services, and was roundly told off for acting like heavies on behalf of big business. The initial response was as uncompromising as Kirchner's opinion of the European companies themselves, which he expressed face to face with them in his July 2003 trip to the old continent, causing widespread anger in corporate circles – he told them that the immense profits they had made in Argentina during the 1990s also had to be taken into account.

The bad news is that the agreement demanded that Argentina produce a primary budget surplus of three per cent of GDP during 2004, which represents a 20 percent increase over 2003. Rather than help reactivate the economy, this surplus must be destined exclusively to debt service. Other targets, such as greater application of the 21 per cent sales tax, have a strong recessionary bias. The agreement also required the government to request that Congress give it the power to unilaterally increase public utility rates, leading many to believe that rate hikes were imminent.

Meanwhile, Kirchner has proved he is a worthy follower of Perón in that he has listened to everyone – an attitude that everybody found disarming. Congress deputy Patricia Walsh, the main mover behind the process to annul the laws of Punto Final and Obediencia Debida, is a combative left-wing politician used to being brushed off. Yet she recounted to journalists how when she approached the new president to impress upon him the importance of her work against impunity, he actually paid attention – and that was how she summed it up for the papers, 'he listened'. The Abuelas, known for their scepticism of politicians, came out of their audience with him cautiously advancing the opinion that perhaps some change was afoot in the corridors of power.

Kirchner has said things which place him squarely in the traditional terrain of the left. Where does this leave the popular movement? For many discontents, the new government presents the chance to leave politics to the politicians once more, as this time there's a 'good guy' in charge. Demobilisation of gatherings such as the neighbourhood assemblies has coincided with his rule, but they were on the wane already, for many other reasons. For those unclear as to what should change in the way the country works, possibly a majority of the population, Kirchner provides a good enough solution.

Yet for those who have taken up social change as a way of understanding the ongoing economic difficulties and the political process that led to crisis, the new president provides new opportunities to voice their demands. Several piquetero groups support Kirchner. He has received piquetero families in the presidential offices and was photographed kissing piquetero children when he signed an agreement providing 1,800,000 pesos (US$640,000) for their microenterprise projects. A member of a radical autonomous MTD who wanted to remain anonymous summed up her group's position: 'If Menem had been elected we were getting ready to leave the country, because repression would have been violent. We don't like Kirchner but he gives us time to strengthen our organisation.'

Perhaps the most surprising thing about Kirchner is the lack of opposition he has encountered. The stiffest resistance has come from those who have taken the biggest losses outside Argentina, namely business interests in Europe. US assets must have done better, given the friendly advice President George W. Bush gave Kirchner to negotiate hard with the IMF. In fact the good disposition Kirchner encountered in the US seems odd considering Washington lost the slavish support provided by Menem. Argentina has refused to send troops to the Middle East, and it voted against the US on Cuba in April 2003, while Duhalde was president.

In Argentina, Kirchner has publicly accused the rich and powerful in Argentina of looting the country with no thought to its future, and he has told the military – to stony silence – that they must re-examine their conduct during the dirty war. And the conservative press and associations have been uncharacteristically quiet since he actually took power. Just before, *La Nación*, the country's main conservative newspaper, published five 'guidelines' for the president-to-be just before he took office: unconditional support for the US, meeting with its ambassador and businessmen, condemnation of Cuba, the rehabilitation of the dirty war and extreme security measures.[3] The interests represented by *La Nación* are critical of Kirchner's actions since he became president, but there is no organised attempt to belittle him, as there was during his presidential campaign. It may be that they haven't worked out a strategy yet, but it is puzzling. Or it may simply be too damaging given the level of support he enjoys now – whatever the reason, it is unlikely to last forever.

The criticisms that have been made of the government have often received immediate and forceful responses from the President, often on TV. It may be that these responses reflect a forced transparency of the political process due to his lack of political machinery. Public opinion via TV is his only recourse, and in the post-Argentinazo era, it also helps to be seen as 'directly' in contact with the people. His style of government has depended on an element of surprise in announcing imminent action, with no overall programme being put forward.

The main criticism levelled at Kirchner's first 100 days in government, from his left and from the right, was that he had no economic programme to bring the country back from its disastrous state. International investors demanded measures to guarantee their freedom, national businesses wanted help, and the majority unemployed clamoured for jobs and social security. The content of his speeches so far has put the wellbeing of society over the interests of the economically powerful, but his actions have been limited. What he has done is change the tenor of discussions, which could be summed up by another quote from his speech at the UN General Assembly. There he said that 'nobody has ever been known to collect any debt from the dead', a not-too-subtle message to the IMF and other creditors. Taking into account the small print of the agreement with the IMF, it can be seen that his rhetoric is better than his praxis. But public support runs high as his behaviour reflects social consensus. That is exemplified by the polls taken just after the deal was struck with the IMF: over 70 per cent thought it was a good result and that the president and the economy minister, Roberto Lavagna, had done well – but 90 per cent thought the agreement benefited the Fund. Argentina has gone from living an illusion to being too 'realistic'.

It is to be hoped that soon they will feel able to demand more. Yet it is hard to see how Kirchner could substantially restructure the economy to fulfil social needs immediately – or indeed whether he would choose to. The reformist agenda he has initiated – of improving tax collection, reducing the value of government debt, investing in state works and continuing the emergency social security measures passed in 2002 – is far from radical. But given the neo-liberal policies implemented over the last quarter of a century in Argentina, he represents a departure from politics as usual.

Notes

1 *Clarín*, May 18 2003
2 *The Economist*, 'Néstor Kirchner's nimble cookery', September 11th 2003
3 Verbitsky, H. 'Los cinco puntos,' *Página/12*, May 18 2003

Glossary

Alianza	Ruling coalition (1999–2001) made up of the Radicals and the FREPASO (see below). In full, the Alianza para la Justicia, el Trabajo y la Educación, the Alliance for Justice, Work and Education, established in 1997
Argentinazo	The popular uprising of December 19th and 20th 2001, mainly in Buenos Aires
Austral	Currency introduced in 1985 and abolished in 1992
Asambleas	Neighbourhood assemblies that began to meet after December 2001
Casa Rosada	Presidential offices on the Plaza de Mayo, central Buenos Aires
Cacerolazo	Demonstration using pots and pans (cacerolas) to make a noise
Cartoneros	People who collect paper and cardboard from waste to re-sell it
CTA	*Central de los Trabajadores Argentinos* Confederation of Argentinian Workers
Convertibility Plan	Decree passed in 1991 whereby one peso became equal to one US dollar
Corralito	Limit on cash withdrawals from bank accounts decreed by Economy Minister Domingo Cavallo on December 1st 2001
Corralón	Freezing of bank account contents and forcible conversion to pesos from dollars at a rate established by the government of Eduardo Duhalde in early 2002
FREPASO	Frente País Solidario, Country in Solidarity

	Front, progressive political party founded in 1994
Madres de Plaza de Mayo	Human rights group founded in 1977 by mothers of those disappeared by state repression
MTDs	*movimientos de trabajadores desempleados,* unemployed workers' movements, radical and autonomous piqueteros
Peronists	Members of the Partido Justicialista (PJ) and their supporters
Plan Jefas y Jefes de Hogar	Heads of household benefit
Plaza de Mayo	Central square in Buenos Aires surrounded by the executive offices, the colonial seat of power (cabildo), the city's cathedral and ministries
Porteños	Inhabitants of the city of Buenos Aires
'Process'	Commonly-used shortened version of 'Process of National Reorganisation', the policy programme implemented by the last dictatorship (1976–1983)
Puebladas	Peoples' rebellions against the established powers
Radicales	Members of the political party Unión Cívica Radical, UCR
Trueque	Barter

Key dates

	Revolution'
1958	civilian president Arturo Frondizi
1962	Military coup and successive military regimes
1966	General Juan Carlos Onganía comes to power; Congress closed; repression against Peronist and other political parties increased
1967	Death of Ernesto 'Che' Guevara
May 1969	Thousands of citizens take control of Argentina's second city, Córdoba, for two days, routing the army and police
1970	Onganía ousted by fellow officers; General Alejandro Lanusse eventually takes over as president
1973	Peronists allowed to stand in elections; their candidate, Héctor Cámpora wins; fresh elections; Perón elected president for the third time, dies a few months later, leaving his widow Estela 'Isabelita' as president
March 1976	Military coup
1976–1983	Period of the *proceso militar*; up to 30,000 people disappear at the hands of the state
1982	Junta leader General Leopoldo Fortunato Galtieri sends troops in April to the Falklands/Malvinas islands; British task force retakes them by mid-June
1983	collapse of military regime; Radical party leader Raúl Alfonsín elected president
1989	Radicals lose presidential elections; amid growing economic chaos, Alfonsín hands over power to new elected President, Carlos Saúl Menem of the Peronist party
1991	Start of economic policy with *peso* at parity with US dollar
1994	New constitution approved, allowing the president to serve two consecutive terms in office
1995	Menem wins second term

1996	Fernando de la Rua elected as first mayor of the city of Buenos Aires
1996	Broad coalition of unions organise two general strikes against proposed law of labor flexibility and government's economic policies
1997	Teacher's union CTERA sets up teacher hunger strikes in front of national congress
1997	the Alianza, an electoral alliance of UCR and FREPASO, formally established
1999	Fernando de la Rua wins the presidential election for the UCR/FREPASO coalition
November 2001	Government responds to a run on banks by limiting access to bank deposits
December 2001	Large segments of the middle class take to the Buenos Aires streets in protest. Supermarket ransacking occurs in poorer neighbourhoods and violent protests in the Plaza de Mayo
	Fernando de la Rua forced to abandon presidential residence, signalling the collapse of his government and an ensuing power vacuum
	Argentina temporarily ceases payment on its foreign debt
January 2002	Eduardo Duhalde selected by Congress to serve as president, after 3 interim presidents step down.
January 2002	Duhalde decrees the end of the parity of the peso to the dollar and freezes bank accounts, forcing conversion into pesos at fixed exchange rate
May 2003	Néstor Kirchner assumes the presidency

Bibliography

Aspiazu, D. (Ed.) 2002, *Privatizaciones y poder económico: la consolidación de una sociedad excluyente.* Quilmes, Universidad Nacional de Quilmes

Auyero, J. 2000, *Poor people's politics: Peronist survival networks and the legacy of Evita,* Durham, Duke University Press

Bielsa, R. et al., 2002 *Qué son las asambleas populares.* Biblioteca del pensamiento nacional. Buenos Aires, Ediciones Continente

Calcagno, A.E and E.Calcagno 2002, *La deuda externa explicada a todos (los que tienen que pagarla)* Buenos Aires, Catálogos

Hora, R. 2001, *The landowners of the Argentina pampas: a social and political history 1960–1945,* Oxford, Oxford University Press

Hunt, L.1996, *Barings lost: Nick Leeson and the collapse of Barings Plc,* New York, Butterworth-Heinemann

James, D. 1994, *Resistance and integration, Peronism and the Argentine working class, 1946–1976,* Cambridge, Cambridge University Press

Jozami, A. 2003 *Argentina: la destrucción de una nación,* Buenos Aires, Mondadori

Lewis, C.M. 2002, *Argentina, a short history,* Oxford, Oneworld

López Echagüe, H. 2002, *La política está en otra parte, viaje al interior de los nuevos movimientos sociales,* Buenos Aires, Norma

McCaughan, M. 2002, *True crimes, Rodolfo Walsh, the life and times of a radical intellectual,* London, Latin America Bureau

MTD Solano y Colectivo Situaciones 2002, *La hipótesis 891: más allá de los piquetes,* Buenos Aires, Ediciones de mano a mano

Nouzeilles, G. and G. Montaldo (Eds.) 2002, *The Argentina reader,* Durham, Duke University Press

Rock D. 1989, *Argentina, 1516–1987: from Spanish colonization to*

Alfonsín, Berkeley and Los Angeles, University of California Press

Romero L. A. 2002, *A history of Argentina in the twentieth century*, University Park, Pennsylvania, Pennsylvania State University Press

Seoane, M. 2003, *El saqueo de la Argentina*, Buenos Aires, Editorial Sudamericana

Thorp, R. 1998, *Progress, poverty and exclusion: an economic history of Latin America in the 20th century*, Baltimore, Johns Hopkins University Press for the Inter-American Development Bank

News in English

Financial Times, www.ft.com/world

Buenos Aires Herald, www.buenosairesherald.com

News in Spanish

Indymedia Argentina, argentina.indymedia.org

Clarín, www.clarin.com

Página/12, www.pagina12.com.ar

La Nación, www.lanacion.com ar

For regularly updated information and online resources, including web details of many of the organisations mentioned in the book, check the Argentina Country Profile at www.lab.org.uk

More titles in this series of short, topical and timely books on current affairs and major issues affecting the region and beyond from the
Latin America Bureau

Politics Transformed: Lula and the Workers' Party in Brazil
Sue Branford and Bernardo Kucinski
Politics Transformed tells the story of the PT's origins and electoral history, outlining their key politicians. It is the riveting story of the four tries for power, culminating in the success of October 2002, when the PT took 62 per cent of the vote and Lula became the first left-wing politician to gain the presidency in Brazil. The book explores how Lula's government will fare in the context of the economic crises and the competing demands for austerity and social justice.

2003
ISBN 1 899365 61 3

The Battle of Venezuela
Michael McCaughan
A timely look at the important events unfolding in Venezuela. Journalist Michael McCaughan paints a vivid picture of Venezuela since Hugo Chàvez came to power, interviewing people of all political classes and opinions in extensive detail. With a solid analysis of Venezuelan history, which helps to place current events, *The Battle of Venezuela* illuminates de role Chávez has played in the political development of contemporary Venezuela and the social forces his Bolivarian revolution have unleashed.

2004
ISBN 1 899365 62 1

Visit www.lab.org.uk and buy our books online, or contact us:
Latin America Bureau
1 Amwell Street
London EC1R 1UL
United Kingdom
t. 44 (0) 20 7278 2829
f. 44 (0) 20 7833 0715
info@lab.org.uk